FIRST LADIES OF THE PARISH

Books by Ruth A. Tucker

From Jerusalem to Irian Jaya
Daughters of the Church (with Walter L. Liefeld)

FIRST LADIES OF THE PARISH

*Historical Portraits
of Pastors' Wives*

Ruth A. Tucker

**Ministry
Resources
Library**

Zondervan Publishing House • Grand Rapids, MI

FIRST LADIES OF THE PARISH
Copyright © 1988 by Ruth A. Tucker

MINISTRY RESOURCES LIBRARY
is an imprint of Zondervan Publishing House,
1415 Lake Drive, S.E., Grand Rapids, Michigan 49506.

Library of Congress Cataloging in Publication Data

Tucker, Ruth, 1945–
    First ladies of the parish : historical portraits of pastors' wives /
Ruth A. Tucker.
        p.   cm.
    Bibliography: p.
    Includes index.
    ISBN 0-310-40431-2
    1. Clergymen's wives—Biography. 2. Evangelists' wives—Biography.
I. Title.
BR1713.T83   1988
253'.2'0922—dc19
[B]   87-28594
                                                                      CIP

Printed in the United States of America

88   89   90   91   92   93 / EP / 10   9   8   7   6   5   4   3   2   1

• Acknowledgments •

The following sources have provided the photographs and illustrations used in this book. Grateful acknowledgment is given for permission to use these items.

Katie Luther, Idelette Calvin: L. Penning, *Genius of Geneva: A Popular Account of the Life and Times of John Calvin* (Grand Rapids: Wm. B. Eerdmans, 1954), 180. Used by permission of Wm. B. Eerdmans Publishing Co.

Katherine Zell: Georges Hirth, *Les Grands Illustrateurs,* 2nd ed. (Munich: Knorr and Hirth, n.d.), 1:41.

Susanna Wesley: *John Wesley the Methodist: A Plain Account of His Life and Work* by a Methodist Preacher (New York: Methodist Book Concern, 1903), 17.

Mary Fletcher: J. Burns, *Life of Mary Fletcher* (London: Joseph Smith, 1853), frontispiece.

Sarah Edwards: Permission from Yale University Art Gallery, Bequest of Eugene Phelps Edwards.

Eunice Beecher: William C. Beecher and Rev. Samuel Scoville, *A Biography of Rev. Henry Ward Beecher* (New York: Charles L. Webster, 1888), 168.

Margaret Simpson: A. E. Thompson, *The Life of A. B. Simpson* (New York: Christian Alliance Publishing Company, 1920), 141.

Emma Moody: William R. Moody, *The Life of Dwight L. Moody* (New York: Fleming H. Revell, 1900), 71.

Susannah Spurgeon: Henry D. Northrop, *Life and Works of Rev. Charles H. Spurgeon* (New York: Memorial Publishing Co., 1892), 24.

Daisy Smith: Hope Evangeline, *Daisy* (Grand Rapids: Baker Book House, 1978), 134. Used by permission of Baker Book House.

Catherine Marshall: Photograph provided by Chosen Books.

Ruth Peale: Helen Marcus, 120 East 75th Street, New York, NY 10021. Copyright © 1977 by Helen Marcus.

Jill Briscoe: Photograph provided by Zondervan Publishing House.

• Contents •

• Introduction •

Pastors' wives have changed considerably in the past decades, as have women in every vocation in life. In an effort to speak to these changes, a steady stream of advice books for pastors' wives has come off the presses: *How to Be a Preacher's Wife and Like It* (1956), *How to Be a Minister's Wife and Love It* (1968), *The Unprivate Life of a Pastor's Wife* (1972), *The Private Life of the Minister's Wife* (1981), *Who Is the Minister's Wife?* (1980), *So You're the Pastor's Wife* (1979), *The Underground Manual for Ministers' Wives* (1974), and *Home Sweet Fishbowl: Confessions of a Minister's Wife* (1982). The list goes on and on. The one thing these books have in common is that the pastor's wife is viewed as a woman who has a unique role to fill and faces frustrations that are unique to her relationship and vocation.

The books likewise show changing attitudes. In 1956, Lora Lee Parrott admonished pastors' wives that "a broom, mop, pail and box of detergent, plus an ample supply of elbow grease, can transform any dingy parsonage into a sparkling set of rooms." She further insisted that "parish obligations should never come ahead of parsonage obligations. Your first responsibility is to provide a clean, well-ordered home for your pastor-husband and your family."[1]

But only two decades later, Jill Briscoe was confessing that an unwary visitor had found "wet tennis shoes, the dog's dishes, and the like" falling out of her "overstuffed corner cupboard."[2] And Karen Mains admitted she has "no compunctions . . . about asking for help with the vacuuming, sending a seminarian upstairs to bathe a baby, giving a pile of potatoes to someone to peel," or putting up guests overnight on the floor and letting them get up and cook the breakfast in the morning.[3]

Yet, despite the changes that have occurred in the role and outlook of pastors' wives, what is more amazing is the continuity over the centuries. Katie Luther, Katherine Zell, and Idelette Calvin—all first-generation Protestant pastors' wives—faced the very same role-related concerns that pastors' wives are facing today. The struggles that confronted Susanna Wesley in the eighteenth century, Eunice Beecher in the nineteenth century, and Daisy Smith during the first decades of the twentieth century are some of the very issues pastors' wives are confronting as the twentieth century comes to a close.

Pastors' wives in every generation have had widely varying views of their station in life. Some have resented the intrusion of the parishioners into their lives and have been exasperated by the long hours required of their husbands. This position was expressed by an Anglican vicar's wife: "Clergy ought to be celibate . . . because no decent, right-minded man ought to have the effrontery to ask any woman to take on such a lousy job! It is thoroughly un-Christian. . . . I myself am happy, basically, because I love my husband—but I am afraid it is often in spite of the 'church.' "[4]

Other pastors' wives, however, have a completely opposite picture of what the life of the parish first lady is like. Alice Taylor, the wife of an Episcopalian minister, writes, "Should this woman who lives in the rectory be pitied? Never. Envied? Yes, for there is no life more rewarding."[5]

Historically the position Alice Taylor represents had been more true to fact. According to historian Leonard I. Sweet, "The nineteenth century saw the minister's wife emerge from the crowd to become the institutional leader of church women and to occupy one of the most coveted careers available to American women." Indeed, he says that "the most common vocational fantasies of Evangelical women in nineteenth-century America involved becoming a minister's or a missionary's wife. Both roles represented lives devoted to soul-winning, and both permitted women a public, assertive form of usefulness."[6]

What is there to be gained by looking at pastors' wives through the perspective of history? Do women of prior generations really have anything relevant to say to women today? They do, and in many respects their lives are more open to scrutiny. It would be difficult to analyze openly and objectively Susanna Wesley's marriage breakdown or Eunice Beecher's pain and humiliation over her husband's widely publicized accusation of adultery if these women were our contemporaries. But peering into their personal lives from a distance allows the reader to identify with the problem, yet not be caught up in the conflict.

Likewise, we learn about the role of women in ministry by using the historical perspective. Is the role changing with the times, or is there a continuity that provides fitting role models for today's women? Surprisingly, there is a significant amount of continuity—particularly in the role that pastors' wives have played over the past five centuries. The same desire for partnership in ministry that Katie Luther longed for is felt today by women for whom marriage to a minister is the highest ideal. Then as now it offers opportunities for ministry that no other religious vocation does.

Looking at other women through history also brings an added perspective to just what a pastor's wife is. A book title states the problem succinctly—*The Minister's Wife: Person or Position?* What are we talking about when we speak of a pastor's wife? Are we simply referring to a person and a relationship, or are we speaking of a role that entails a vocational ministry?

There has been debate for centuries as to whether the Reformation served to open or close the door of ministry for women. Roman Catholics have argued that the Protestants sought to shut the door by closing convents and denigrating the life of a celibate nun; Protestants have maintained that the cloistering of nuns did not allow for effective ministry anyway. It is true that the Reformation Protestants did not offer women full-time professional ministries, but by discarding the requirement that the clergy be celibate, they opened a new avenue of ministry for women in the role of the pastor's wife. Indeed, among those select few who were married to ministers, there were outstanding women who turned that role into a vibrant Christian ministry.

The position then as now, however, was filled with problems and struggles. In fact, the difficulties were magnified due to the fact that the position had not yet been legitimized. Nor were there any role models for those first pastors' wives. Here were women venturing without precedent into a ministry frontier. Some shrank from their opportunities; others were seemingly spurred on by the obstacles they confronted.

As important as their ministry was, and as much as Protestants would argue that the Reformation did not close the door, pastors' wives have been more obscure than women in other areas of ministry. When great preachers have excelled, they have been the subject of biographies and have been included in church history texts. The biographies of preachers' wives, however, are few and far between. Those that do exist are written about women whose husbands (or sons, in the case of Susanna Wesley) excelled in the ministry. The adage "Behind every great man is a great woman" may have some truth, but it is unfortunate that the "great woman" is forgotten while the man is heaped with adulation.

The question also arises whether these men were really so great. Yes, they achieved great success—in many cases founded great movements, built great churches, presided over great religious campaigns, delivered great sermons, and wrote great books. But they were not always great husbands and fathers, and they sometimes failed miserably in their spiritual lives. Indeed, they were not the "super-saints" we often envision them to be, and this perspective is often seen most clearly when their lives are glimpsed through the eyes of their wives. Denise Turner captures the reality with a humorous touch: "Maybe some ministers can fool all of the people all of the time, but the minister who can fool his own wife is yet to be born."[7]

What about the "great women" behind these great men? Were they a species of spiritual giants that has now become extinct? They, too, had their failings. Sometimes they moaned about their lot in life instead of going out and ministering to others in more difficult circumstances, and sometimes they failed to appreciate their husbands' visionary outlook. But despite their shortcomings, they made significant contributions to the ongoing progress of the Christian faith—contributions that have too often been forgotten.

The pastors' wives discussed in this volume represent a variety of denominations. From Idelette Calvin to Jill Briscoe, they represent a cross section of Protestantism. Some of their husbands were Calvinists, some Arminians; some were fundamentalistic, some were more liberal. As is typically true of women, however, they were generally not overly concerned about theological distinctions. They focused primarily on ministry, and thus they were affected less by fine points of doctrine than their husbands were. They differed from each other in their roles and in their different responses to challenges and problems in the ministry. Their social backgrounds varied, as well as their relationships with their husbands and the people in their parishes. Yet these women had much in common, and I have a suspicion that if all fourteen of them were somehow miraculously brought together on a Tuesday morning in Jill Briscoe's living room, they would have so much to talk about that the conversation and chatter would still be going strong when Stuart arrived home after a late-night church committee meeting.

As a former pastor's wife, I identify with these women. I have known the frustration of trying to carve out a role that will meet the expectations of the parishioners. And I have experienced many of the problems these women faced and have known the inner conflict of not being able to share these difficulties with anyone else. But I have also enjoyed the challenges that come with the territory—the satisfaction of having a young person seek me out for counsel *because* I am the pastor's wife, the fulfillment in helping plan the church's first annual missions conference, the satisfaction of hearing a sermon illustration from a magazine article that I shared with my husband.

As I reflect on those years, my deepest regrets are not the problems in the parish, but the problems in my own life. If I had one overriding inadequacy, it was immaturity—a characteristic that permeated every aspect of my ministry. At twenty-seven I was certainly not among the very youngest of pastors' wives, but I am convinced I was among the least mature. I sought too much to identify with teenagers (and am horrified as I look back at the photos of my stylish short skirts of the early 1970s). I was too quick to speak my mind, too slow to appreciate the traditional values of the "old-timers." I was too defensive of my husband and not affirming enough of other people's gifts.

Part of my problem was that I had no training for the position. I was busy with my own graduate studies and erroneously believed I did not have time to study such inconsequential matters. I had not read one book on the topic and had taken no classes or even attended a seminary wives' meeting. The opportunities were there, but I was too arrogant to realize my desperate need for them.

It is with this hindsight that I offer this volume. It is not a book of advice from my own experience, but a compilation of the experiences of many pastors' wives. It is a collage portrait of the pastor's wife, and it is a volume that would have helped me immensely before and during my years as "first lady of the parish."

I suspect that the problems and challenges of the pastor's wife today and in the future will not be less complicated than they were for me. Indeed, I have a hunch that fulfilling that difficult role will become progressively complex for women in the years to come. Columnist Ellen Goodman has some provocative thoughts on first ladies, and though she is speaking of Presidents' wives, the same could be said for pastors' wives:

> Let me just say that increasingly we expect these highly visible women to do SOMETHING, but nothing controversial. We expect them to be SOMETHING, but nothing that overshadows their husband. . . . We don't elect first ladies. . . . They . . . come with the territory. But the way we accept spouses may be particularly important. It may determine how many new couples get into the running.[8]

Yes, it is true that parishioners, if they wish to attract a capable and well-qualified pastor, are going to have to reevaluate their attitude toward the pastor's wife and allow her to develop her own style of ministry within the parish. She "comes with the territory" and thus is an important part of the parish community, but she must have freedom to be herself. This, then, is a book not just for pastors' wives, but also for parishioners—that they might develop an appreciation for the varied styles and ministries of pastors' wives through the centuries and today.

· PART I ·
MINISTRY ROLES

Finding a fulfilling role as a pastor's wife that does not cause controversy among the parishioners is not an easy task in today's world. There are no seminary degrees that prepare people for the profession of clergy spouse—or more appropriately, pastor's wife—and thus women often flounder in their efforts to find ministry in a less than professional but more than lay capacity. Because the pastor's wife is not employed by the church and there is no job description per se, she is often frustrated and finds it, in Denise Turner's words, "so easy to fall into the trap of trying to fill the shoes of the previous minister's wife, even if those shoes don't fit. Most likely, the previous minister's wife did the same thing with the shoes of the one before her too."[1]

The qualifications of a pastor are clearly spelled out, and a church board or congregation can determine on the basis of specific criteria whether or not he is competent enough to fill the position. For the pastor's wife, who is likewise expected to demonstrate competence in a variety of areas of ministry, there are no set qualifications. "I had certainly not been required to demonstrate any musical talent when I applied for a license to marry a minister," writes Denise Turner. "I didn't even have to pray out loud in front of the county clerk. Later, of course, I did hear that piano-playing could be a real plus, and I promptly brushed up on my scales."[2]

What, then, is the proper role for pastors' wives, and what ought to be their job description? A quick glance at three first-generation pastors' wives indicates that from the very beginning there was room for latitude. Katie Luther was an independent and energetic woman when she got married, and she remained so as a pastor's wife. She was deeply involved in her husband's ministry and in offering hospitality to visitors of every stripe at their spacious manse, but she did not let that prevent her from becoming heavily involved in business matters outside the parish ministry.

Katherine Zell, on the other hand, was wholly taken up with parish work and other ministry duties. She gave sanctuary to refugees and made their needs known to civil officials; she aided the sick and the poor in the parish and the surrounding community; she wrote letters, edited hymn books, and conducted funeral services when duty demanded.

Idelette Calvin's ministry was distinct from both Katie Luther's and Katherine Zell's. While they catered to the needs of their husbands and took their domestic responsibilities seriously, they did not devote themselves to care and support of their husbands to the extent that Idelette did. Attending her husband's needs was her top priority, and though she was sickly much of the time, Calvin's ministry was enhanced by her devotion.

Katie Luther, Katherine Zell, and Idelette Calvin all provide models for women today who are serving in the parish with their husbands in the capacity of pastors' wives. Their lives reflect different emphases in ministry that are as valid today as they were in the sixteenth century.

KATIE LUTHER

• 1 •
Katie Luther
Enjoying a Career
in Nonparish Ministry

A pastor's wife who is independent enough to have a vocation or business outside the church is considered by many to be a woman who is reflecting the modern trend for women that has corresponded with late twentieth-century feminism. Indeed, the trend toward outside employment for pastors' wives has become so common that many churches simply accept the issue as routine. "Large numbers of ministers' wives," writes Denise Turner, "report that they encountered no interference whatsoever from their churches when they decided to seek employment outside the home. Of course some do; and it should also be said that the minister, himself, occasionally turns out to be a rather formidable obstacle."[1]

Yet, despite the obstacles, more and more clergy wives are working outside the home. In 1980, statistics indicated that 51 percent of them were employed, which was a higher percentage than was seen in the general population. Economic considerations were a major factor, but career fulfillment was also a significant reason for outside employment. A controversial aspect of the wife's work is how it influences her husband's ministry—particularly "the traditional primacy of the clergy 'call.' The replies of the ministers indicate that 50 percent of them would be influenced on relocation by their wife's employment."[2]

Some pastors' wives themselves take a strong stand against involvement in a secular vocation. Frances Nordland writes,

> It is my personal opinion that in most instances it would be better if the minister's wife did not seek outside employment. If she is employed, she cannot share as fully in the life of the church and in certain ministries of her husband. She will not have time for Bible study and prayer that will contribute to a rich spiritual ministry of her own.[3]

But those who would decry the independent pastor's wife who has vocational activities outside the parish need to be reminded that Katie Luther, who laid the foundation for Protestant pastors' wives, was frequently occupied with work outside the church.

This was true during a time when women had very little opportunity to demonstrate any independence apart from the men in their lives. A woman was under the control of her father until she married, and then she was under the control of her husband. At the time of the Reformation, a woman had virtually no say in her destiny or the customs that defined her existence, as Katie's childhood and marriage illustrate.

It is a scene that would create scandal in the 1980s—especially if it involved the pastor and his new bride. The scene is their bedroom on their wedding day. The bride and the bridegroom are in bed, surrounded by friends of the groom who are there to witness the consummation of the marriage. Here was the most private and intimate moment in this woman's life being invaded by curious onlookers. It was a scene that no doubt humiliated the bride, Katie Luther, as it must have all sixteenth-century brides. The men apparently saw it differently. Justus Jonas, Martin Luther's good friend, described the scene the following day: "I was present yesterday and saw the couple on their marriage bed. As I watched this spectacle I could not hold back my tears."[4]

One wonders if Katie had difficulty holding back the tears as well. She had spent much of her life in a convent, and it is difficult to imagine her in such an intimate situation with bawdy men standing around. Yet it was this scene that inaugurated a new era in women's ministry, for on that memorable day Katharine von Bora Luther became Protestantism's first pastor's wife. Some historians might argue that Luther was not the first Protestant clergyman to marry, but to Katie Luther, nevertheless, goes the title of "First Lady of the Reformation."

As the first pastor's wife, Katie Luther paved the way for women in all denominations who would find themselves struggling with their own identities in the shadow of the pulpit. Like those who were to follow, she faced problems and controversies unknown to women in other careers. It was essential that this ministry be recognized in its own right and that the pastor's wife did not become merely an appendage of the pastor. Moreover, Katie had to define a ministry that had never before existed. What is the job description for a pastor's wife? Is it actually a job, or is it merely a relationship? Should she be expected to be more involved in the church than, say, a deacon's wife? It was up to Katie to lay the groundwork and set the stage for women who like herself would aspire that noble calling but would encounter great frustration in fulfilling it.

Katharine von Bora was born in 1499 in a little village near Leipzig. Her parents enjoyed a certain degree of financial security, and Katie, unlike the vast majority of girls in the early sixteenth century, received an education, and that beginning at a very early age. Before the age of six she began her studies at a Benedictine school, and after her mother died and her father remarried, she was sent away to a Cistercian convent to be prepared for solemn vows. Her early education and convent training was no doubt influenced by two aunts from both sides of the family—one who served as abbess of the convent where she took her vows, and another who later escaped the convent with her.[5]

As a nun, Katharine von Bora had surreptitiously learned of Martin Luther's teachings while living at the Cistercian convent of Nimbschem. She was one of forty cloistered nuns who had almost no contact with the outside world. Even relatives who came to visit were separated from the nuns by a latticed window, and an abbess was present to overhear the conversations. The rule of silence was upheld, and nuns were not permitted to form friendships among themselves. They were even instructed to have their heads lowered as they walked around the convent.[6]

In spite of the strict supervision, Luther's writings had penetrated the walls of the convent. For some of these nuns, the daring writings brought excitement and flights of fantasy about life outside the barren convent walls. Such a fantasy was fulfilled in 1523, when Katharine and eleven other nuns secretly made arrangements to escape. Their struggle in accomplishing that end illustrates the problem nuns faced in many parts of Germany and elsewhere in Europe. Their convent was located in an area controlled by Duke George, a staunch enemy of the Reformation—a man who regarded "kidnapping" nuns as a capital offense. The nuns sent word to Luther of their plight, and despite the personal risk involved, he made arrangements for their escape. The story is familiar. Luther arranged to have a merchant who sold smoked herring to the convent make the delivery late at night and on his return trip to bring out the nuns instead of the empty herring barrels.[7]

It was an ingenious coup, but it only added to the many frustrations already confronting Luther. What to do with the nuns was the most immediate problem facing him. Some were able to return to their families, but the rest would need more than just temporary lodging. The problem was addressed by a cynical student in Wittenberg who reported, "A wagon load of vestal virgins has just come to town all more eager for marriage than for life. May God give them husbands lest worse befall."[8]

Finding husbands for these nuns was a difficult assignment, and Luther became perturbed with the slow process. "Katherine was something of a problem, because she was too proud and too particular in her choice of a husband, not being satisfied with any of the suitors found for her. Although already past the marriageable age of girls in that day, she was immediately popular with the younger Wittenberg crowd." It was one of these young men, Jerome Baumgaetner—the son of a renowned family in Nuernberg—who won her heart. They fell in love, and he began making plans for their wedding in Nuernberg. "But in his youthful enthusiasm he had forgotten to consider the position of his parents. This proud family would hardly approve of a runaway nun as daughter-in-law." Jerome never returned for his bride, and Katie was so heartbroken that she became physically ill.[9]

Luther was also upset. He thought he had one less nun to worry about, but his plans had been foiled. He made a final effort, however, to rectify the situation. In the fall of 1524, he wrote to the young man:

> If you still wish to hold your Kathie von Bora, you had better act fast before she is given to another who is at hand [Dr. Kaspar Glatz]. She still has not conquered her love for you. I would certainly be happy to see you two married. Farewell.[10]

Luther's urgent appeal to Jerome may have been prompted by his fear that Katie would scorn any effort to marry her to Kaspar Glatz, an older man who was described as miserly. She did object, and she made her case very clear to Nicholas von Amsdorf. She called on him and "protested that Luther was trying to force her to marry Glatz, whom she detested. She knew that Luther and Amsdorf were close friends, and she boldly added that if Luther or Amsdorf were willing, she would readily arrange an honorable marriage with either, but with Glatz, never."[11]

How Luther reacted to the proposal is unknown, but it is a well-known fact that he had not seriously contemplated marriage for himself. During the very time he was seeking to arrange Katie's marriage he had written to a friend who had enquired about his own prospects for marriage: "Hitherto I have not been, and am not now inclined to take a wife. Not that I lack the feelings of a man (for I am neither wood nor stone), but my mind is averse to marriage because I daily expect the death decreed to the heretic."[12]

Only months later, however, after Katie's interview with Amsdorf, Luther was seriously contemplating marriage. A motivating factor might have been a visit to his parents' home and the strong encouragement they gave him to marry. He followed through with that advice in the summer of 1525, when he was forty-two and Katie was twenty-six. Virtually nothing is known of his and Katie's courtship. Indeed, there may never have actually been one. Luther later advised that "it is very dangerous to put off your wedding, for Satan gladly interferes and makes great trouble through evil talkers, slanderers, and friends of both parties." In reference to his own marriage he wrote, "if I had not married quickly and secretly and taken few into my confidence, everyone would have done what he could to hinder me; for all my best friends cried: 'Not this one, but another.'"[13]

How secure Luther was about his relationship with Katie before their marriage is uncertain. He later admitted that he was not in love with her at that time—a factor that is not terribly significant in light of the times. Romantic love was not a prerequisite for marriage. Luther's choice of Katie was a great disappointment to some of his close associates. Philip Melanchthon reportedly despised her, remarking prior to the marriage, "marry, yes, but for heaven's sake not that one."[14]

Katie's not-so-subtle suggestion that Luther marry her may have been prompted by her desire to marry someone who would be actively involved in ministry. In that sense she no doubt believed she would be an appropriate wife for him. Indeed, like so many young women today, she desired that special type of ministry that could only be acquired through marriage to a pastor. She saw in marriage to Luther a partnership in Christian ministry that could not be equaled otherwise. But despite her apparently pure motives, she struggled with acceptance from the very beginning.

Melanchthon's criticism was mild compared to that coming from the religious opposition. Some Roman Catholics were convinced that their union would surely produce the Antichrist. Even more than her husband, Katie was singled out as a subject of scorn. A pamphlet, published two years after their marriage, denounced her in scathing terms:

> Woe to you, poor fallen woman, not only because you have passed from light to darkness, from the cloistered holy religion into a damnable, shameful life, but also that you have gone from the grace to the disfavor of God, in that you have left the cloister in lay clothes and have gone to Wittenberg like a chorus girl. You are said to have lived with Luther in sin. Then you have married him, forsaking Christ your bridegroom. You have broken your vow and by your example have reduced many godly young women in the cloisters to a pitiable state of body and soul, despised of all men.[15]

Did Luther and Katie actually "live together in sin," as some of the rumors suggested? According to Melanchthon, they did not. He knew Luther well and was angered by his fear that, in marrying, Luther "waxes wanton and diminishes his reputation, just when Germany has especial need of his judgment and authority." It was too late, however, to make amends: "Now that the deed is done, we must not take it too hard, or reproach him; for I think, indeed, that he was compelled by nature to marry." But to the issue of sexual promiscuity, Luther was blameless: "The rumor, however, that he had previously dishonored her is manifestly a lie."[16]

Facing such accusations was a distressing ordeal for a young pastor's wife, especially at a time when there was no precedent for her role and ministry. It was likewise difficult to hear the vicious attacks against her husband, who had sacrificed so much for the cause. Yet she was not a passive observer during the tumultuous early years of the Reformation. Rather, she was an independent, strong-willed, feisty redhead who was not afraid to speak her mind. On one occasion Luther reportedly commented that "the only way to get an obedient wife was to hew her out of stone," and he confessed that at times he played the role of a "willing servant" to his "Lord Kathe."[17]

Despite her struggles and personality flaws, Katie served with distinction as the mistress of the first Protestant parsonage. She had a calming influence on her husband—an influence Melanchthon had hoped would make a noticeable change. Though he had strongly opposed the marriage, once it was accomplished, Melanchthon sought to see it in the best light possible. To a friend he wrote of Luther, "I have hopes that this state of life may sober him down, so that he will discard the low buffoonery which we have often censured."[18] Marital love, no doubt, mellowed Luther considerably. "I would not change Katie for France or for Venice," he wrote, "for God has given her to me and other women have worse faults." According to Roland Bainton, she "ministered to her husband's diseases, depressions, and eccentricities. She had great skill with diet, herbs, poultices, and massages."[19]

In some respects Katie should be viewed as a model preacher's wife for all times. She was a gracious hostess to hundreds of house guests over the years, not only seeing that their physical needs were cared for, but also making them feel welcome. "She came to be the mistress of a household, a hostel, and a hospital. The Augustinian Cloister, where Luther had lived as a monk, was first loaned and then given to the couple by the Elector. It had on the first floor 40 rooms with cells above. The day was to come when not a single room was unoccupied." She delegated work, however, and thus was not constantly tied down with menial tasks. In fact, she often joined Luther as he talked with refugees and students who had come for counsel, and her congeniality and wit were a source of encouragement.[20]

The Luther parsonage was truly a lively center of activity. "Where formerly sedate monks had walked about by twos with bowed heads and sober mien, dressed in the somber black robes of the order, the halls now echoed the laughter and chatter of children's voices, the hustle and bustle of a busy household, the vitality and exuberance of youth." Luther and Katie had six children, and they became a deep source of pride to Protestants who still had painful memories of their Catholic past and the outward requirement of clerical celibacy. "When little Hans, the eldest, arrived on June 7, 1526, it was a day of great rejoicing for Luther's friends all over Germany," and "the arrival of the first tooth at six months was a national event."[21]

In addition to their own children, the Luthers welcomed other permanent and temporary residents—a situation that was described in a letter to the German prince, who had been contemplating a visit to the Wittenberg parsonage:

> The home of Luther is occupied by a motley crowd of boys, students, girls, widows, old women, and youngsters. For this reason there is much disturbance in the place, and many regret it for the sake of the good man, the honorable father. If but the spirit of the Doctor Luther lived in all of these, his house would offer you an agreeable, friendly quarter for a few days so that your Grace would be able to enjoy the hospitality of that man. But as the situation now stands and as circumstances exist in the household of Luther, I would not advise that your Grace stop there.[22]

Yet, despite her large home and constant stream of visitors, Katie was not tied to the parsonage. Besides their home in Wittenberg, she operated a small farm at Zuhlsdorf (previously owned by her family), and on occasion was away from Wittenberg for days or weeks at a time. She was a highly versatile woman—a fact that Luther himself acknowledged in letters to her when he spoke of her as his "gracious Miss Katherine Luther of Bora and Zuhlsdorf" and as the "preacher, brewer, gardener, and all things else."[23] On other occasions he had referred to her as "my Kind and dear lord and master, Katy, Lutheress, doctoress, and priestess, of Wittenberg." Yet again, ten years after they married, he had this description: "My lord Kate drives a team, farms, pastures, and sells cows . . . and between times reads the Bible."[24]

This outside activity prepared Katie for her life as a widow. Luther died suddenly in 1546, leaving her with young children to provide for. Although he had received a very adequate salary when he was alive, it was consumed in daily expenses. "He had accumulated some property, but it did not provide ready revenue. Now Kathie needed her gifts for management as never before." Her financial plight, however, was not her most pressing problem. Keeping her family together was. A government official was determined that her sons should be removed from the home for their schooling. She fought hard to keep them, and in the end she prevailed.[25]

Katie's financial problems worsened when military strife wreaked havoc on her farm in Zuhlsdorf and her other properties. "Her livestock had disappeared, barns and sheds had been pillaged and burned. To rebuild the farms she borrowed a thousand gulden and resumed the boarding of students." In 1552, during an epidemic of the plague in Wittenberg, she had a serious accident in her horse carriage while in a rush to get out of town. She hung on to life for some months, but died shortly before Christmas in 1552, at the age of fifty-three. Her four surviving children ranged in ages from eighteen to twenty-six.[26]

Katie Luther serves as a role model for those pastors' wives who are struggling for acceptance and striving to identify their own particular ministries. She likewise demonstrated how a pastor's wife can have a life outside the church, and she showed that a spirit of independence can be a valuable asset—especially when her source of support is suddenly taken from her.

KATHERINE ZELL

Katherine Zell
Pursuing a Personal Parish Ministry

Women have always been on the forefront of humanitarian services, and that has been particularly true of women in the church. They have initiated mission endeavors of all kinds and have rallied their sisters to the cause. Pastors' wives have been exceptionally visible in this area of ministry, both inside and outside the parish.

"Ministers' wives worked with church women for a variety of missions," writes Leonard Sweet. "Sometimes they dispensed charity—fuel, clothing, food, seldom money—to the poor. Sometimes they packed food, furniture, quilts, and clerical shirts for 'indigent but pious' seminary students." Sometimes they supported "wornout preachers." Indeed, they performed a wide variety of functions from supporting missionary efforts to fund-raising for new church buildings. "The wife of an Ohio Presbyterian minister, James Hoge, responded to Columbus's cholera epidemic in the 1830s by forming the city's longest-lived charitable organization." These and countless other examples show the important role the pastor's wife played in outreach to some of society's most needy people.[1]

Very often the ministry to needy people takes place in the parsonage itself. In her book *Open Heart, Open Home,* written while her husband was a pastor in Chicago's inner city, Karen Mains tells of her ministry of hospitality to many people who were often unable to reciprocate. The book offers refreshing insight into the life of a pastor's wife—so different from the majority of books that emphasize the problems and disappointments that come with the position. "For ten years my husband and I have lived in Chicago's inner city or close to it," she writes. "We have immersed our lives in the needs and problems of its inhabitants. Ours is a fractured society much in need of healing. . . . Christ's ministry to this impoverished, captive, blinded and oppressed world must, in one way or another, also be ours."[2]

Offering hospitality to those who could not reciprocate and going out into the community to serve the needy formed Katherine Zell's primary ministry. Katherine was very different in many ways from Katie Luther, who stood in the shadow of her larger-than-life husband. Had Katie not been married to the most conspicuous man of the Reformation, she may never have made a lasting mark on the annals of church history.

Not so with Katherine Zell. She was an activist who was recognized as a Reformer in her own right. Although her ministry was tied to that of her husband, Matthew Zell, a Catholic-priest-turned-Lutheran-preacher, Katherine's deep interest in spiritual values developed long before she married him. In fact, her spiritual pilgrimage began more than a decade before Luther nailed the Ninety-five Theses to the church door in Wittenberg. "Ever since I was ten years old I have been a student and sort of church mother, much given to attending sermons. I have loved and frequented the company of learned men, and I conversed much with them, not about dancing, masquerades, and worldly pleasures but about the kingdom of God."[3]

Matthew Zell's marriage, like Luther's, was highly controversial, and in 1524 the bishop suspended the clerical privileges of all married priests. This action infuriated Katherine, who was well aware of the lifestyle of the celibate ministers, who were often accused of seducing young women and girls. She defended her own role by arguing that marriage to a priest was a ministry that diminished the moral degradation of the clergy, and she accused the church of having financial considerations in preventing such marriages.[4]

As a pastor's wife, Katherine's primary ministry involved hospitality and service to Protestant refugees and travelers, some of whom were well-known Reformers of the day. Many, however, were ordinary people who needed temporary shelter while fleeing persecution in Catholic-controlled regions. During one three-week period she provided room and board in the parsonage at Strasbourg for some sixty homeless victims of religious persecution. "Her zeal is incredible for Christ's lowliest and afflicted," a Protestant leader wrote of her. Strasbourg was a "free city"—not controlled by the imperial government of Austria—and thus it became a center for refugees fleeing the brutal atrocities of religious persecution.[5]

The depth of Katherine's concern for religious refugees was seen not only in her feeding and housing them, but in her consideration for their families left behind. She wrote a tract in the form of a letter to be distributed to wives who were anxiously waiting to learn their husbands' plight. In it she sought to give words of encouragement by reminding them of Scripture verses. For many of these women who did not have access to the Bible, this tract may have become a priceless treasure:

> To my fellow sisters in Christ, day and night I pray God that he may increase your faith that you forget not his invincible Word. "My thoughts are not your thoughts, saith the Lord" (Isa. 55:8). "Whom I make alive I kill" (Deut. 32:39). The Lord would wean you from the world that you may rely only on him. Has he not told us that we must "forsake father and mother, wife and child"? (Luke 14:26). "He who denies me him will I deny in the presence of my father" (Matt. 10:33). "Those who would reign with me must also suffer with me" (2 Tim. 2:12).
>
> Had I been chosen to suffer as you women I would account myself happier than all the magistrates of Strasbourg at the fair with their necklaces and golden chains. Remember the word of the Lord in the prophet Isaiah (54:8) "In overflowing wrath for a moment I hid my face from you, but with everlasting love I will have compassion on you. . . ."[6]

During the Peasants' War of 1525, Katherine became even more involved in relief work. She had initially focused her attention on peace efforts and accompanied her husband and another leading minister of the area to the military camps to plead with the two sides to lay down their arms. "The pleas went unheeded and the peasants were massacred. Survivors together with the wives and children of the slaughtered, flocked into Strasbourg to the number of 3,000." Katherine directed much of the relief work, enlisting the aid of others for the massive effort.[7]

But even in the selfless task of aiding refugees, Katherine became embroiled in controversy. She did not limit her kindness to those with whom she agreed on minor theological points, stating emphatically that "anyone who acknowledges Christ as the true son of God and the sole Savior of mankind is welcome at my board."[8]

Not only did Katherine forcefully answer her critics, but she went on the offensive, attacking their bigotry. "Why do you rail at Schwenckfeld?" she demanded of a Lutheran leader. "You talk as if you would have him burned like the poor Servetus at Geneva. . . . You behave as if you had been brought up by savages in a jungle. The Anabaptists are pursued as by a hunter with dogs chasing wild boars. Yet the Anabaptists accept Christ in all the essentials as we do."[9]

Katherine was conversant with some of the greatest Protestant leaders of the Reformation. In 1529, Ulrich Zwingli, the great Reformer from Zurich, visited in Strasbourg for two weeks and stayed in the home of Matthew Zell. He was "hospitably entertained by his wife Catharine," writes historian Philip Schaff, "who cooked their meals, waited at the table, and conversed with them on theology so intelligently that they ranked her above many doctors."[10]

Some years later Calvin visited the city. While he was there he became embroiled in a theological and personal controversy with some other ministers. In an effort to resolve the matter, "he was taken to the home of the ever reconciling Zells. There, as he later confessed, Calvin blew up disgracefully until he was mollified. How much Katherine had to do with the cooling we do not know. She was the hostess." Soon after that, Katherine and her husband took a trip themselves, at which time they journeyed some six hundred miles to visit Martin Luther and Philip Melanchthon in Wittenberg.[11] Whether or not Katherine and Katie Luther were able to share their struggles and joys as pioneer pastors' wives is not recorded, but if they did they surely must have had much to discuss.

Katherine was an outstanding pastor's wife, considering the countless hours and tireless energy she poured into the ministry of the parish. This may have been due in part to the fact that she was childless—two babies died shortly after birth—but her commitment to the Reformation was far deeper than a need to fill her life with activities. In the absence of motherly duties, "she was free to devote herself to the self-appointed role of serving as her husband's helper."[12] After the untimely death of her husband, she continued to function in her role as a pastor's wife—a servant to needy refugees—for a decade and a half.

Her activism and outspoken criticism of the Protestant religious establishment made Katherine Zell more than suspect as a pastor's wife. Indeed, she was apparently so much a threat to the Lutheran clergy in Strasbourg that she felt obliged to speak at her husband's funeral, assuring her listeners that she did not seek to become "Doctor Katrina," as rumor had it. "I am not usurping the office of preacher or apostle," she insisted. But she was not about to be stifled altogether. "I am like the dear Mary Magdalene, who with no thought of being an apostle, came to tell the disciples that she had encountered the risen Lord."[13]

Katherine was a strong woman. Unlike so many of her female contemporaries, she believed in herself. She was determined that she would not be relegated to an unfulfilling and unchallenging existence simply because she was a woman. But she was also deeply sensitive. The criticism and misunderstanding of her ministry, combined with the overwhelming grief over her husband's death, proved to be too much for her to endure with composure. Her world caved in around her, and it became evident that she needed rest and solitude. Friends arranged for her to stay in the home of a pastor in Switzerland, and Martin Butzer, a renowned Reformer of the day, sent along a letter of introduction. Among other things, he reflected on her character: "The widow of our Zell, a godly and saintly woman, comes to you that perchance she may find some solace for her grief. She is human. How does the heavenly Father humble those endowed with great gifts!"[14]

Katherine apparently made a swift recovery from her collapse. In less than a year after her husband's death she was back in

Strasbourg, and from the tone of her letters she was as involved in her ministries after his death as she had been before it. Her concern for needy refugees and displaced Protestant leaders continued. To one of these leaders she wrote, "I am sending your wife and your daughter-in-law each a pound of flax for spinning shawls. I would have sent more if I had had a carrier. I have been allowed to keep the parsonage which belongs to the parish. I take any one who comes. It is always full. I don't know how long I can keep it."[15]

The quick return to her demanding ministry did not by any means eliminate the depression Katherine suffered with the death of her husband. In a letter to two Protestant Reformers, whom she had helped to hide from authorities, she apologized for her lack of hospitality: "I wish I could have done better for you but my Matthew has taken all my gaiety with him." In that same letter she rebuked the men for having left behind two gold pieces for her. "You put me to shame to think that you would leave money for me, as if I would take a *heller* [small copper coin] from you poor pilgrims and my revered ministers." She returned one of the coins, knowing they would need it. She would have returned the other as well, "but a refugee minister has just come in with five children, and the wife of another who saw her husband beheaded before her eyes. I divided the one gold piece between them as a present from you."[16]

Some years after her husband's death, Katherine was again obliged to defend her ministry—this time against charges of disturbing the peace. Again she gave a sharp response:

> A disturber of the peace am I? Yes indeed, of my own peace. Do you call this disturbing the peace that instead of spending my time in frivolous amusements I have visited the plague infested and carried out the dead? I have visited those in prison and under sentence of death. Often for three days and three nights I have neither eaten nor slept. I have never mounted the pulpit, but I have done more than any minister in visiting those in misery. Is this disturbing the peace of the church?[17]

Katherine's ministry involved more than charitable work for the needy. She also compiled hymns and published them in pamphlet form in an effort to focus the minds of laypeople on God more effectively. Her motivation illustrates the depth of her own spiritual maturity:

> When I read those hymns I felt that the writer had the whole Bible in his heart. This is not just a hymn book but a lesson book of prayer and praise. When so many filthy songs are on the lips of men and women and even children I think it well that folk should with lusty zeal and clear voice sing the songs of their salvation. God is glad when the craftsman at his bench, the maid at the sink, the farmer at the plough, the dresser at the vines, the mother at the cradle break forth in hymns of prayer, praise and instruction.[18]

Besides hymns, Katherine also published and distributed tracts, often filled with Scripture references of encouragement to people suffering hardship and persecution. She also used her gift of writing in more personal ministries. When a city official who was a longtime acquaintance of hers was quarantined from Strasbourg because he had contracted leprosy, she visited him and spoke to local magistrates about improving his situation. She also wrote to him, and one of these writings later appeared in tract form. It was a letter of reassurance and consolation that could be applied to many situations:

> My dear Lord Felix, since we have known each other for a full 30 years I am moved to visit you in your long and frightful illness. I have not been able to come as often as I would like, because of the load here for the poor and the sick, but you have been ever in my thoughts. We have often talked of how you have been stricken, cut off from rank, office, from your wife and friends, from all dealings with the world which recoils from your loathsome disease and leaves you in utter loneliness. At first you were bitter and utterly cast down till God gave you strength and patience, and now you are able to thank him that out of love he has taught you to bear the cross. Because I know that your illness weighs upon you daily and may easily cause you again to fall into despair and rebelliousness, I have gathered some passages which may make your yoke light in the spirit, though not in the flesh. I have written meditations on the 51st Psalm: "Have mercy upon me, O God, according to thy loving-kindness," and the 130th: "Out of the depths have I cried unto thee, O Lord," and then on the Lord's Prayer and the Creed.

Katherine's "meditations" on Scripture were brief and to the point. They were designed not to be scholarly commentary, but to be a practical source of encouragement to a downcast soul.[19]

One of Katherine's final acts of selfless service was conducting a funeral service for a woman disciple of the radical reformer Kaspar von Ossig Schwenckfeld. A Lutheran minister had agreed to conduct the funeral, but only with the stipulation that he publicly renounce the woman for denying the faith. Her husband refused and instead called upon Katherine, now old and feeble, to conduct a graveside service at dawn so as to avoid the authorities. Later the city council voted that if Katherine recovered from her illness, she would be duly reprimanded. She did not.[20]

Even before she became a pastor's wife, Katherine profoundly understood the necessity of such a ministry. She was outspoken, and she challenged authorities—not because she was a feminist of her day, but because she was so absolutely convinced of her calling that she would allow nothing to deter her. Indeed, her role as a pastor's wife had become so much a part of her identity that it effectively continued long after her husband died.

IDELETTE CALVIN

Idelette Calvin
Serving in a Supporting Role

Since the onset of the modern feminist movement, the concept of a wife serving in a supporting role to her husband is not a popular notion. Even many pastors' wives, who are expected to be the perfect embodiment of a supportive spouse, are challenging the concept. Others, however, are suggesting that such a role is the most important one a pastor's wife can play in her ministry in the parish. Gail MacDonald, the wife of Gordon MacDonald, the well-known minister, author, and Christian leader, champions this kind of supportive role for a pastor's wife. "I am probably more active in our congregation than the wives of a lot of pastors," she writes. "But my activity within the congregation is carefully limited because I saw long ago that my greatest ministry to our church would be in the provision of a home for their pastor. If I did my job at home, he would be able to come refreshed each day to serve the people who had called him to be their spiritual shepherd."[1]

Betty Coble would concur with Gail MacDonald. In her advice to the pastor's wife, she makes a strong case for the kind of role she should expect to maintain.

> Her most important area of church service is to provide a close, honest, relationship with her husband. She should not assume a personal responsibility for all the church needs. She is to be a person

who cares for, prays for, and relates to her husband; and on other occasions she ought to contribute a female point of view. Her best contribution in many situations is to be a good listener.[2]

Idelette Calvin personified many of these characteristics. She saw her role as one primarily in support of her husband, and she filled that role well.

For the first generation of Protestants, marriage was a far more significant decision than it was in the generations that followed. Renouncing celibacy was viewed by the Catholics as giving in to the sin of lust, and because of that perception, some of the Protestant leaders felt it was more appropriate if they remained single. In writing to one such individual, Calvin offered his own position on the subject, stating explicitly what he viewed to be the role of the pastor's wife: "I whom you see so opposed to celibacy am not yet married. Whether I shall ever marry I do not know. In any case, if I take a wife it will be in order that, freed from many cares, I can consecrate myself to the Lord."[3]

When John Calvin married Idelette, he did not have stars in his eyes. He knew precisely what kind of a wife he wanted, and in her he was convinced he would find those necessary qualities. In his active search for a wife, he had written to his friend William Farel and had clearly spelled out his specifications.

> But always keep in mind what I seek to find in her; for I am none of those insane lovers who embrace also the vices of those with whom they are in love, where they are smitten at first sight with a fine figure. This only is the beauty which allures me, if she is chaste, if not too fussy or fastidious, if economical, if patient, if there is hope that she will be interested about my health.[4]

Idelette was not the first woman Calvin had intended to marry. At the age of thirty, after serving for some years in pastoral work in Geneva and Strasbourg, Calvin had made arrangements to be married. To Farel he had written, "We look for the bride to be here a little after Easter." The woman he had in mind was apparently a wealthy supporter from Germany, whose brother was serving as a go-between. On the one hand, her financial status was strongly in her favor, as Calvin had confessed: "I cannot call a single penny my own. It is astonishing how money slips away in extraordinary expenses." On the other hand, he was concerned about how his marrying into wealth would appear to others: "You understand, William, that she would bring with her a large dowry, and this could be embarrassing to a poor minister like myself. I feel, too, that she might become dissatisfied with her humbler station in life." Because of these and other factors, the marriage never took place.[5]

Farel suggested his own choice of a wife for him, but Calvin apparently was unimpressed by the fact that she was fifteen years older than he was. Calvin found another candidate on his own, and again he contacted Farel, to make sure that he would be prepared to come and officiate sometime not "beyond the tenth of March." Though he was hopeful this arrangement would work, Cavin confessed his uncertainty: "I make myself look very foolish if it shall so happen that my hope again fall through." And that is precisely what happened.[6]

So discouraged was Calvin in his inability to find a wife that he lamented to Farel, "I have not found a wife and frequently hesitate as to whether I ought any more to seek one." But amid that discouragement, he discovered the ideal wife in his own congregation. Idelette was a young widow with two children. She and her husband had been Anabaptists who were converted to the Reformed faith through Calvin's preaching. In the spring of 1540, while Calvin was in the process of arranging the second time for marriage, Idelette's husband had died of the plague, and so she was available to become the pastor's wife Calvin was seeking. In August, only months after her husband died, they were married.[7]

As much as Calvin had hoped that marriage would improve his financial circumstances, that was not the case. Idelette's children comprised her only "fortune," and they would bring only added burden to him financially. But more important, Idelette was a patient and loving woman, and that is exactly what Calvin needed to counter his own "impatience and irritability."[8]

From the beginning, her marriage to the great Reformer was filled with complications and frustrations. In addition to his pastoral work in Strasbourg, Calvin was a teacher and houseparent at his own boarding school. Home for Idelette and her children thus became the boarding school, which was governed to a significant degree by a domineering and often caustic housekeeper. For the quiet and retiring Idelette, it was a threatening situation. To make matters worse, both she and her husband became ill shortly after their marriage. "As if it had been so ordered," wrote Calvin, "that our wedlock might not be over joyous, the Lord thus thwarted our joy by moderating it." Sickness would plague them throughout their marriage.[9]

Calvin's residence in Strasbourg had begun after a harrowing twenty-month pastorate in Geneva. He did not consider himself first and foremost a pastor. He was a scholar and a writer, and his tenure at Geneva had come only after his friend Farel had pleaded with him to stay on after a one day's visit. Geneva was a needy city, and Calvin desperately sought to reform it. Some accused him of trying to establish a theocracy through the strict laws he sought to enforce. The city council cooperated on some matters, but among the citizenry, the opposition was unrelenting. They defied his efforts to control their social and religious activities. After one tense council meeting, an angry mob was waiting outside. When Calvin and Farel emerged, the crowd spit and shouted obscenities and threatened them with physical violence. That night Calvin was kept awake by gunshots and pounding on his door. "This was all a nightmare to the shy twenty-eight-year-old Frenchman, at his desk with quill and flickering candle. He jumped with every shot and with every boot that kicked the door."[10]

After Calvin refused to offer communion to these people on Easter Sunday in 1538, he and Farel were both ordered out of town. "Well and good" summed up Calvin's response. Things were considerably more peaceful in Strasbourg—until Calvin began receiving strong pleas for him to return to Geneva. Some of the council members and citizens who had previously opposed him had had a change of heart. Farel, too, begged Calvin to return to his city. Calvin was adamant: "Rather would I submit to death a hundred times than to that cross, on which one had to perish daily a thousand times over." But the pressure became too great to resist, and in 1541, three years after he left, Calvin returned to Geneva, leaving Idelette behind until he was convinced that Geneva was truly the place where he could remain and raise a family.[11]

So grateful was the Geneva city council that Calvin was willing to return that they gave him gifts, including a "new robe of black velvet, trimmed with fur," and they "passed a resolution stating that a messenger of state be dispatched to bring with him Idelette 'and her household.' In this manner she received honors befitting a royal princess." No longer would she be living in a student boardinghouse. The church provided them with a home—a former abbey—on Rue de Chanoines, near the cathedral and somewhat secluded from their neighbors, with a lovely view of Lake Geneva and the towering Alps. Along with some serious reservations, she arrived in Geneva with her children in a two-horse carriage.[12]

Idelette had clearly become "first lady" of the parish, and she could have enjoyed a lifestyle that might have been vastly different than what she had previously known. But she chose otherwise.

> Idelette, if she had chosen, might have passed her time in presiding over brilliant social gatherings. But like her unostentatious husband, she devoted her time and energy for the most part to the performance of charitable duties. She often visited the sick, the poor, and the humble folk. On many occasions she entertained visitors from communities who sought inspiration from her husband.[13]

Most of Idelette's time was spent at home, caring for the needs of her husband and children and the extended family that sometimes included her brother and sister-in-law and nieces and nephews. She managed to put meals on the table by tending a garden in the backyard and through the additional salary her husband was paid because of his heavy household expenses.[14]

As a preacher Calvin had no time for frivolity. Preaching God's Word was serious business, and if the townspeople expected him to reflect on his departure and return to Geneva on his first Sunday back, they were grossly mistaken. His style was to preach expository sermons going from one chapter or portion of Scripture to the next, Sunday after Sunday. Although he had been away for three years, he methodically started exactly where he had left off, with no reference to the time that had intervened.[15]

Calvin would not have returned to Geneva if he had not been absolutely assured that things would be different and that he would be accorded greater respect than he had received previously. But neither was he blind to the problems he would encounter. There were confrontations with city leaders who feared he was again attempting to assume dictatorial powers. His most bitter enemies, however, continued to be the Libertines, who opposed his puritanical regulations on community social life.[16]

In addition to the stress created by the continual opposition to her husband, Idelette had to endure ugly personal slander. Françoise Favre and other Libertines in Geneva, who despised Calvin's strict authoritarianism, "spread the word that Idelette was a woman of ill repute and that her two children had been born out of wedlock." The story was true only to the extent that she and her first husband—in a situation typical among Anabaptists who regard marriage as a sacred religious vow that should be made before God alone—were not married in a civil ceremony. Thus in the eyes of the law they were never officially married. Some suggested that for this sin, God was punishing Calvin and Idelette in not giving them children of their own. This charge was interesting in light of Calvin's belief that marriage, as God had planned it in the Garden of Eden, had only one purpose: procreation.[17]

It was certainly not that the Calvins did not try to have children. In fact, Idelette became pregnant three times, but none of the children lived beyond infancy. Soon after coming to Geneva, Idelette gave birth to a boy, but baby Jacques was sickly and lived only two weeks. Three years later a baby girl was stillborn, and two years after that another child was dead at birth.[18]

At the birth of Jacques, Idelette became very ill, and his death only added to her physical anguish. The following month, Calvin wrote a friend, sending greetings from his wife, whom he said was unable even to dictate a letter of appreciation for their kindness. And then Calvin added, "The Lord has certainly inflicted a severe and bitter wound in the death of our infant son."[19]

Despite her chronic ill health and the pain of losing three little ones, Idelette took seriously her role as the wife of Geneva's eminent preacher. His name was becoming a household word among first-generation Protestants, and there were many visitors who sought his attention. "Your hospitality in the name of Christ is not unknown to anybody in Europe," wrote an acquaintance some years after they had settled in Geneva. Although Calvin received the letter and was given the tribute, it was Idelette who provided the home atmosphere that made his hospitality possible, and it was her stabilizing influence that helped him to maintain his hectic schedule of pastoral duties, writing, and receiving visitors. "No one knows," writes Thea Van Halsema, "how often the quiet sympathy and loving care of Idelette brought peace to the busy intense man who was her husband."[20]

Unlike Luther, Calvin rarely spoke of his family in his letters or other writings, and thus his domestic life has remained something of a mystery to historians. Whether he grew to love his stepchildren as he would have his own is unknown, but during her last, debilitating illness, Idelette apparently seemed unsure of his commitment to their care should she die. Because the concern for her children was adding to her distress, Calvin sought to alleviate her fears: "Since I feared that these personal worries might aggravate her illness, I took an opportunity, three days before her death, to tell her that I would not fail to fulfill my responsibilities to her children."[21]

The children were approaching adolescence when she died, and they would have been expected to care for their own needs. Their environment in Geneva, apart from the religious atmosphere of their home and church, offered many worldly pleasures, and without their mother's close supervision they no doubt found it difficult to resist the temptations. Several years after Idelette died, her daughter Judith was convicted of adultery. So humiliated was Calvin over the scandal that he refused to leave the house for days.[22]

Today, in an age of advanced medical specialization, intensive care units, and various kinds of life-prolonging technology, few people give serious thought to the subject of having a "holy death." But for Christians in prior generations, a holy death was of utmost importance. Biographies of the saints always include a spiritually uplifting final chapter on the individual's passing. So it was with Idelette Calvin.

As the hour of Idelette's death approached in 1549, Calvin expressed his parting thoughts to her: "I said a few words to her about the grace of Christ, the hope of everlasting life, our marriage and her approaching departure. Then I turned aside to pray."[23] Calvin later spoke of her peaceful composure on the day she died, the tranquillity interrupted only by her personal tribute to God:

She suddenly cried out in such a way that all could see that her spirit had risen far above this world. These were her words, "O glorious resurrection! O God of Abraham and of all of our fathers, the believers of all the ages have trusted on Thee and none of them have hoped in vain. And now I fix my hope on Thee." These short statements were cried out rather than distinctly spoken. These were not lines suggested by someone else but came from her own thoughts.[24]

When she died, Calvin wrote of his deep sorrow, and he gave some insight into what Idelette had meant to him as a wife: "I have been bereaved of the best companion of my life, who, if our lot had been harsher, would have been not only the willing sharer of exile and poverty, but even of death. While she lived she was the faithful helper of my ministry. From her I never experienced the slightest hindrance."[25]

Idelette proved to be the very wife John Calvin needed. Some might have considered her a poor choice because of her poor health and the children she left behind for him to raise. Surely he might have accomplished more without the weight of family responsibilities. Yet it was Idelette who added softness to what otherwise tended to be a harsh, authoritarian ministry. This quality of tenderness, far more than those possessed of a geriatric nurse, was exactly what Calvin needed. She gave him children— though they were not his own—who helped him to understand the realities of life. Even the disgrace his stepdaughter later brought upon him showed him that as much as he had preached against sin, he and his family were certainly not immune from the temptations of the world.

Calvin never remarried. After Idelette's death, he vowed "to henceforth lead a solitary life."[26] He did not view this vow sanctimoniously. Indeed, he was convinced that if God wanted him married, it would be a sin to remain single; but he was apparently convinced that God had given him an "infirmity" that made him unsuitable for marriage: "I know my infirmity, that perhaps a woman might not be happy with me."[27] So John Calvin lived out his solitary life, with only his fond memories of his dear wife Idelette.

· PART II ·
MINISTRY PROBLEMS

According to one author, "being a pastor's wife is the most hazardous and dangerous occupation a woman can have," and "only the best adjusted emotionally, those who have had full love and security in childhood, and who are thick-skinned will ever come through the experience emotionally and mentally unscarred."[1] That is a harsh judgment, but it often reflects the reality for the first lady of the parish.

Many of the books written for pastors' wives focus to a significant degree on ministry problems. A quick glance at the table of contents in Frances Nordland's book, *The Unprivate Life of a Pastor's Wife,* illustrates this. Chapter titles include "Feelings of Inadequacy," "Conflicts Related to Time, Energy and Children," "Reject Self-Pity," "Finances," "Tensions and Fatigue," "Stress and Strain," "Loneliness," and "Jealousy."

Book titles also reflect the problems a minister's wife faces: *Clergy Couples in Crisis, Coping With Stress in the Minister's Home,* and *What's Happening in Clergy Marriages?* Most pastors' wives do not have to be reminded that their role encompasses many problems—problems that are common to the general population, but that pastors' wives are not supposed to have. It is this factor that adds complexities to their ministry and makes their situation unique.

"By far the greatest suffering of the consecrated minister's wife," writes Dorothy Pentecost, "comes from feelings within her that cannot be expressed to others, not from external things, such as the work expected of her, or the difficulties encountered with the conditions in the manse, or even the financial sacrifices entailed." She goes on to say that "many a pastor's wife may smile beautifully on the congregation at church meetings and yet be carrying a broken heart. In spite of giving her all to the work, she is painfully aware of the fact that she is not measuring up to what is expected of her. When she is pleasing one group, she is alienating another."[2]

Historically pastors' wives have struggled with these problems and feelings even as they do today. Susanna Wesley spoke in her personal letters of the anxiety she felt over her husband's domineering attitude in their personal relationship and his subsequent abandoning of her and the children. This was not a matter she could share with other women in the parish; it was a burden she carried deep inside.

Mary Fletcher's adversity was known by all. She had lost her husband—her beloved and trusted companion in ministry. A gloom settled on her life, but she forced herself back into the work despite her sorrow, and her most effective ministry was accomplished during her widowhood.

For Sarah Edwards, being a parish first lady meant enduring a continual series of petty complaints. Her finances, her fashion, and her religious fervor were all a matter of gossip and innuendo. She likewise suffered the consequences of having to relocate after her husband was forced to resign his long pastorate.

The most gossiped about and most dreaded nightmare that any pastor's wife can endure is a charge of sexual immorality against her husband. It was a scandal of this nature that Eunice Beecher encountered, and to make matters worse, her husband was one of the best-known preachers in the country. The story was front-page news for weeks on end.

The problem Margaret Simpson faced made her appear to be an unsympathetic and hostile wife in the eyes of many of her husband's followers, and for that reason she had an added affliction to cope with. Her husband, the prophetic visionary, neglected family matters for a cause he regarded as far more urgent, and

Margaret was often left with heavy family responsibilities without financial means or moral support. She complained of this, and for that she was censored. Like so many of her sisters, she often suffered in silence, taking the innermost trials of her untold story to the grave with her.

SUSANNA WESLEY

• 4 •
Susanna Wesley
Managing a Manse
With Marital Problems

Marriage breakdown is a fact of life in the parish. No matter how evangelical or conservative or fundamentalistic a congregation may be, marital crises are not unheard of in the modern-day church. But despite this growing problem, it is still assumed by many that the pastor and his wife are above such adversities. "It became more and more clear to us," write David and Vera Mace, "that very little is known about the marriages of ministers and their wives. . . . Behind the front they are compelled to put up for the sake of appearance, many clergy couples have very mediocre relationships."[1]

Marital breakdown may be caused in part by the "changing role of women," writes Denise Turner. Today women are more conscious of their own gifts and abilities and are convinced that God leads and speaks to and through them—perhaps as much as through their minister-husbands. Some involved in a ministry outside the church resist the idea of relocating to another area of the country simply because the husband feels he is following God's "call." The real issue, Turner says, is, "Can the minister and his wife work out their differences, make the necessary compromises, and block out any undue interference from their church . . . or will they just decide to split?"[2]

The changing role of women is only one factor related to marital breakdown among pastors and their wives. According to Martha Shedd, an author and minister's wife, "Lots of ministers are not good husbands. They don't put their wives and families first—ahead of other less important business." Another factor involved in marriage breakdown "is the dilemma of facing the mid-life crisis, often in combination with financial troubles, overwork, and feelings of inadequacy."[3]

Susanna Wesley struggled with some of these issues nearly three centuries ago. She was caught up in the dilemma of what her own role should be in conjunction with that of her husband's, and she struggled with a husband who was often insensitive to her needs and those of the family, and who may have been confronting a midlife crisis.

Some women, because of their personality traits and intellectual interests, struggle with life's uncertainties and inequities more than others. This was certainly true of Susanna Wesley. In many ways she was simply born ahead of her time. The spirited independence that so characterized her youth and adulthood brought on difficulties that the vast majority of women during the late seventeenth and early eighteenth centuries never had to deal with.

Most teenage girls of that era, for example, would never have dreamed of challenging family religious beliefs, especially if the father was the parish minister—and a Nonconformist at that. Yet, according to Susanna's biographer, "Before she was thirteen years of age she had carefully sifted the tenets of her father's belief. She had weighed them in the balance against the doctrines of the Established Church and had decided in favor of the church."[4]

Most ministers of that day would have censured a teenage daughter for having dared to challenge long-held theological beliefs. But Samuel Annesley was not an ordinary preacher. On many issues he disputed the accepted beliefs of the day, and women's education was one such issue: "I have often thought of it as one of the most barbarous customs in the world, considering us a civilized and a Christian Country, that we deny advantages of learning to women."[5]

Susanna's proclivity for independent thinking did not subside with her marriage to Samuel Wesley. Like her, he had turned away from the views of his father, who was a Dissenting minister, but that, it seems, was where their similarities ended. Susanna was an aggressive, organized, and strong-willed woman who was patient with her children and tolerant of other people's views. By contrast, Samuel lacked that iron will, had difficulty getting along with people, was inept in money management and business affairs, and was often stubborn and intolerant in his interpersonal relationships.

Indeed, Samuel Wesley was lacking many of the qualities so necessary in the pastorate, and his relational difficulties with parishioners caused emotional stress for Susanna, who was often caught in between. Her ministry style, characterized by encouragement and understanding, was vastly different from his. He rigidly enforced church discipline with little apparent concern for individual circumstances and needs. This created deep resentment and tension in the community and church. Samuel's enemies were many, and Susanna and the children often suffered for it. According to her biographer, "They burned his flax crop, taunted the Wesley children, pried the hinges off the rectory doors. They stabbed his cows so that they gave no milk and once even tried to cut off the legs of the house dog." During the local elections of 1705, the situation became even worse. The Wesley home was surrounded by angry armed townspeople. Soon after that, Samuel was arrested for failure to pay a debt to one of his parishioners and was sent to debtors' prison.[6]

Even before this humiliating incident, however, Samuel had been away from his parish for an extended period of time. On that occasion it was a result of a family dispute, specifically a political disagreement. Susanna, who viewed the Stuarts as the only legitimate line of royalty, considered William of Orange a usurper of the throne. This personal political conviction suddenly became ensnarled with the issue of wifely submission when Susanna refused one evening to say "amen" to her husband's prayer for King William III. In Samuel's mind, his wife had overstepped her bounds—a defiance that required drastic action. "We must part," he insisted, "for if we have two Kings, we must have two beds."[7]

Susanna later recalled the incident. After calling her to his study, "he immediately kneeled down and imprecated the divine vengeance upon himself and all his posterity if ever he touched me more or came into a bed with me before I had begged God's pardon and his, for not saying amen to the prayer for the King." For Susanna, the die was cast.[8]

After that incident, Samuel left home. It was a difficult time for Susanna and the children, but she confessed her true feelings about the situation. "I am more easy in the thoughts of parting because I think we are not likely to live happily together." Furthermore, she was firmly convinced that the fault lay with him, not herself: "I have successfully represented to him the unlawfulness and unreasonableness of his Oath; that the Man in that case has no more power over his own body than the Woman over hers; that since I am willing to let him quietly enjoy his opinions, he ought not to deprive me of my little liberty of conscience."[9]

Samuel returned home after the death of King William III. The political difference that had separated them had been removed, and it was during the period of reconciliation that John Wesley was conceived. Until he was later sent to debtors' prison, Samuel remained in the home most of the time; but it was Susanna who assumed the majority of the home responsibilities. These included maintaining the farm provided by the parish and offering home schooling to her children. She was a dedicated mother—the "supermom" of all times—and she viewed child rearing as a grave undertaking. Indeed, she was exceptionally close to her children. Here her organizational skills were used effectively. She set aside an hour a week in private consultation for each of her children. Each had a specified time, and in later years John reflected on that time with his mother as being a meaningful aspect of his childhood memories.

Susanna also set aside time for her own spiritual development—"a thrice daily period of meditation and reflection"—and she would have spent more time in personal devotion had time permitted. When she was in her early forties and "had buried several times more children than most people have today, and was now in the process of rearing the nine still living," she wrote in her journal:

> Were I permitted to choose a state of Life, or positively to ask of God anything in this world, I would humbly choose and beg that I might be placed in such a Station, wherein I might have daily bread

with moderate care without so much hurry and distraction; and that I might have more leisure to retire from the world, without injuring my [husband] or Children.[10]

But since she did not have a choice, she accepted her "hurry and distraction" as part of God's will and sought to have as much influence on her children's lives as possible.

Susanna was deeply concerned about her children's spiritual well-being. She enquired of them regarding their relationship with God, and even after her sons went to Oxford, "they still regarded their mother as their theological mentor. The letters exchanged between Susanna and son John, for example, reveal his eagerness continually to seek out and attend to her wise counsel, even when it contradicted his own ideas."[11]

It was this counseling that sometimes led to conflict with her husband—with whom, by her own testimony, she rarely agreed. One such incident occurred when John was a student living away from home. He had written to his parents expressing his desire to become ordained and enter the ministry. Samuel advised him to do further study first. Susanna strongly disagreed. Although she had often suggested books for him to read—particularly devotional classics—she deeply feared that the higher theological education would only serve to draw him away from God. "Mr. Wesley differs with me," she wrote, "and would engage you, I believe, in critical learning. . . . I earnestly pray God avert that great evil from you of engaging in trifling studies to the neglect of such as are absolutely necessary."[12]

Susanna's spiritual influence went far beyond her own family. In later years, John referred to her as "a preacher of righteousness"—and for good reason. He quoted a letter she had written to Samuel when he was away during the winter of 1711–12. While she recognized that "as . . . a woman" and "also mistress of a large family . . . the superior charge of souls" was his responsibility, yet in his absence she felt obligated to serve as a spiritual guide.[13]

Initially Susanna's involvement was confined to her own family and neighbor children, but that quickly changed, though not through a concerted effort on her part. "Other people's coming and joining with us was merely accidental. Our lad told his parents: They first desired to be admitted; then others that heard of it, begged leave also: so our company increased to about thirty; and it seldom exceeded forty last winter." Her initial passivity, however, turned into a zealous passion to affect spiritual growth among the people who had sought her out. And what about the sex barriers? "Though I am not a man, nor a Minister, yet if my heart were sincerely devoted to God, and I was inspired with a true zeal for his glory, I might do somewhat more than I do."[14]

Nevertheless, Susanna, aware of a woman's place, kept the meetings confined to her home, but she could not prevent the spontaneous growth that continued unabated. "With those few neighbors that then came to me, I discoursed more freely and affectionately. I chose the best and most awakening sermons we have. And I spent somewhat more time with them in such exercises, without being careful about the success of my undertaking. Since this, our company increased every night; for I dare deny none that ask admittance." This defensive tone was apparently necessary. As a woman, she had to make it clear that she was not overtly seeking a congregation to listen to her renditions of "awakening sermons." Growth continued to the point where she could say: "Last Sunday I believe we had above two hundred. And yet many went away, for want of room to stand."[15]

Perhaps it is not surprising that Samuel questioned his wife's activities. He certainly had never experienced such popularity among his parishioners. At any rate, Susanna felt obliged to answer his concerns for his own reputation with strong convictions of her own.

> I cannot conceive, why any should reflect upon you, because your wife endeavors to draw people to church, and to restrain them from profaning the Lord's day, by reading to them, and other persuasions. For my part, I value no censure upon this account. . . . As to its looking peculiar, I grant it does. And so does almost any thing that is serious, or that may in any way advance the glory of God, or the salvation of souls.[16]

Yet, despite her defense, Susanna had her own reservations "because of my sex." She wrote, "I doubt if it is proper for me to present the prayers of the people to God. Last Sunday I would fain have dismissed them before prayers; but they begged so earnestly to stay, I durst not deny them." In fact, she would have gladly had a man read the sermon, but none was literate enough to do so. Clearly she, like so many women before her, was not making a stand for women's rights, but rather felt compelled to preach the Gospel.[17]

Susanna would not have gone ahead with public ministry had her husband absolutely forbidden her to do so. This was clear when he had earlier objected to her having prayer meetings in the kitchen of the parsonage. In response to his letter of reproof, she wrote, "If you do, after all, think fit to dissolve this assembly, do not tell me that you desire me to do it, for that will not satisfy my conscience; but send me your positive command, in such full and express terms as may absolve me from all guilt and punishment."[18]

It is peculiar that Susanna's preacher-husband would object to these spiritual endeavors that she was involved in, but approve of far more questionable activities. After she had taken a vow never to "drink above two Glasses of any strong Liquor at one time" and was later questioned whether even that was too much, she let her friends and family know, so as to "prevent temptation." But her husband "absolved" her from the vow "as soon as he heard it."[19]

Susanna Wesley would have gladly stood in the shadow of her husband and worked behind the scenes, but when circumstances required that she assume a leadership role, she met the occasion with dignity and humility. Her call to ministry, like that of pastors' wives before and since, was not something she could take lightly. She was compelled to go on even when her husband failed.

The marital breakdown that occurred in the Wesley household took its toll on the family. Though the family is remembered for its two famous sons, Susanna gave birth to nineteen children—only ten of whom survived to adulthood. Susanna poured her life into the children, giving the three sons—Samuel, John, and Charles—their early years of education and her seven daughters their only formal education.

Despite her best efforts, the daughters did not go on to meet Susanna's high expectations, perhaps in part because of the marital turmoil they had seen in their own home and their father's attitude toward women. "Their father," writes Rebecca Harmon, "was sadly lacking in his understanding of women, their needs or their sensibilities. . . . The careers of his sons were his daily concern, but his daughters were in a different category and always took second place." Yet "he loved his daughters after his impractical fashion, but by our criteria he was cruel and unfeeling toward them."[20]

Emilia was the oldest daughter, and she deeply resented her father, lashing out at him in letters to her brothers and blaming him for the "intolerable want and affliction" the family faced financially. She did not marry until she was in her forties, and when she did, it was a poor choice. Her husband abandoned her and their small child a few years after their marriage.

Susanna, the second daughter to survive to adulthood, married a man whom her mother described as "little inferior to the apostate angels in wickedness." Their marriage lasted long enough to produce four children, but eventually they separated.

Molly, the next daughter, was born with a disability. She had one happy year of marriage before she died at age thirty-nine.

Hetty, the fourth daughter, ran away with a man who falsely promised to marry her. Having "ruined" her reputation, she hurriedly married a man she hardly knew, probably "to legitimize a baby she was expecting in less than four months." Her husband became a heavy drinker and treated her cruelly, and she had a miserable life with him.

Nancy was the only daughter who had a long and happy marriage.

Martha, the second to the youngest of the daughters, married a minister who was highly recommended by her brothers. They had ten children before he ran off to the West Indies with a mistress.

Kezzy, the youngest of the girls, never married, but she "was no less pathetic a figure than most of her sisters." After a painful love affair with the scoundrel who later married her sister Martha, she fell in love with a man and became engaged. But Kezzy became ill and died at the age of thirty-two before they were able to marry.[21]

So, while Susanna Wesley is remembered best because she was a devoted mother who knew how to raise children effectively, it was her sons John and Charles who gave her that reputation— surely not her daughters. She is not remembered for her devoted service to the parish. Had that been her only contribution to the church, she would have been lost in obscurity like so many other pastors' wives of ages past. No, she is remembered as a mother—a mother of two of Christianity's most gifted men. Truly she was one of the great mothers in history, but she was far more than a mother. She was a minister—a first lady of the parish par excellence—and that is the way she ought to be remembered.

LIFE

OF

MRS. FLETCHER:

WITH

A BRIEF SKETCH

OF

THE CHARACTER OF HER BELOVED HUSBAND,

THE REV. JOHN FLETCHER,

OF MADELEY:

TO WHICH IS ANNEXED,

SEVERAL OF THEIR LETTERS,

WITH SELECT

Beauties from his Writings.

By J. BURNS,

MINISTER OF ÆNON CHAPEL, ST. MARYLEBONE,

AUTHOR OF "YOUTHFUL PIETY," "THE CHRISTIAN'S DAILY PORTION," "DEATH-BED TRIUMPHS," ETC., ETC.

LONDON:

JOSEPH SMITH, 193, HIGH HOLBORN.

MDCCCLIII.

TITLE PAGE OF BIOGRAPHY

· 5 ·
Mary Fletcher
Surviving the Trials
of Widowhood

The "profession" or "vocation" of pastor's wife is dependent on a relationship. Without a pastor, there is no such thing as a pastor's wife, and thus when death removes the pastor from ministry, it also removes his wife—unless the wife has established herself in the parish to such an extent that her ministry is essential to the welfare of the congregation. Because her identity is so merged with her husband's in all aspects of parish and personal life, the pastor's wife who becomes a widow faces a devastation beyond that of losing a mate. Her ministry that was so bound up with his loses its focus, and if she is living in a church-owned residence, her very day-to-day existence becomes uncertain.

"One of the major decisions faced by the clergy widow arises if she and her husband lived in church-provided housing," writes Charlotte Ross. "She must move, there is no choice." Ross points out, however, that "the clergy widow of today usually has better provisions made for her" than was the case in earlier generations. But no matter what financial provisions are made for her, her ministry as she knew it, for all practical purposes, is over. There are two choices for her future: "To cherish and cling to her role as a clergy wife or to strike out in new and exciting directions."[1]

Striking out "in new and exciting directions" may be the

"right" path to follow, but it is easier said than done. In some instances, clinging to the "role as a clergy wife" may provide the most fulfilling opportunities for future ministry. Such was the case for Mary Fletcher.

Susanna Wesley was only one of many women who had a powerful impact on Methodism. There were countless other women, especially in the early years, who devoted their lives to God through this movement, some of whom John Wesley depended on heavily for preaching and teaching ministries. One such woman was Mary Bosanquet, who later married one of Wesley's most trusted associates, John Fletcher. She became a Methodist class leader when she was eighteen, at the request of John Wesley himself, and continued to serve in that capacity until she was in her mid-seventies.[2]

Mary Bosanquet Fletcher's close association with Wesley lasted to the end of her life. It was a working relationship, but it also involved a deep personal friendship. In a letter to her in 1786, Wesley wrote, "When I receive letters from other persons, I let them lie, perhaps a week or two, before I answer them: But it is otherwise when I hear from you. I then think much of losing a day, for fear I should give a moment's pain to one of the most faithful friends I have in the world."[3] Mary's love and respect for him were equally strong, and she often sought his counsel.

Mary was born in England in 1739, into an upper-class family whose descendants were French Huguenots. From her staunch Anglican father she learned her catechism, but as a youth, having come in contact with some Methodists, she began to have serious questions about the lifestyle in which she was being raised. She objected to theatergoing and to the lavish parties and vacations her family enjoyed. She vowed to forsake such, insisting that she wear the plainest clothes and refusing to participate in worldly amusements. This, not surprisingly, created tension in the home, especially when she refused to agree to her father's demands that she not seek to convert her younger siblings to her brand of Christianity.[4]

Because of these family problems, Mary left home at age eighteen, with a large inheritance she had received from her grandmother's estate, and moved into an apartment to live independently—a shocking course of action at a time when young women lived with their families until they married. She had turned down a marriage proposal from a young man that would have suited her parents' tastes, preferring rather to focus her attention on Christian ministry. She immediately made the acquaintance of John Wesley and established friendships with Methodist women, and soon she was heavily involved in Methodist volunteer work. Of her dear friend, Sarah Ryan, she wrote, "Our hearts were united as David and Jonathan's. The spirit of community that reigned in the church at Jerusalem, I felt a taste of."[5]

Two years after she separated from her parents, Mary was granted possession of her grandmother's estate, the Cedars, which was located in the town of Leytonstone. What could she do with such a large home? Amid a growing social awareness, it did not take Mary long to find a solution. She and Sarah Ryan teamed up to establish a children's orphanage and school—to provide a loving Christian family atmosphere for some of London's homeless, most destitute children. For eighteen years they worked together in this ministry, and in addition they organized a Methodist society in Leytonstone. As was often the case when new societies were formed, there was harsh criticism and bitter hostility from townspeople. A mob congregated in front of the Cedars, "pelting the departing worshippers with dirt, peering in the windows, and 'howling and roaring like beasts in anguish.'" At times the two women feared for their lives, but they were convinced they were where God wanted them to be.[6]

During her busy years with the orphanage, Mary had little time to think about marriage. In fact, she was resigned to the prospect of remaining single—except for those times when she reflected on an acquaintance, John Fletcher, whom she had met during her earliest days of initiation into Methodism in London after leaving home. In her diary she had written, "I had no other thought but of devoting myself to God in a single life; only, I remember, I sometimes thought, were I to be married to Mr. Fletcher, would he not rather be a help than a hindrance to my soul."[7]

Though a strong supporter of Methodism, Fletcher was an Anglican priest, who had served for many years as the vicar of the Madeley parish. He had established himself as a writer and theologian of Methodism, and was widely known for his deep personal piety and holy living. During their early acquaintance Fletcher had contemplated proposing to Mary, and in fact had written to Charles Wesley about the matter; but he failed to act on his instincts, fearing that she might not turn out to be a good wife, and even if she did, she might detract from his love for God.[8]

Mary confided in her diary during those early years of her interest in Fletcher, but she too had reservations that marriage might hinder her ministry—as it undoubtedly would have at that time in her life. Later on, her thoughts of Fletcher occurred more frequently, especially during her last years of ministry with the orphanage, when her inheritance had dwindled and she was facing financial hardship. Marriage, she reasoned, might alleviate her financial concerns, but her hopes were dashed when she learned of Fletcher's serious illness.

Mary had enquired of John Wesley about him, and that may have prompted Fletcher to write to her. Whatever the motivation, Fletcher's letter arrived after there had been fifteen years without any personal communication between them. After two months of correspondence, Fletcher made arrangements to visit Mary, and a few months later, in the fall of 1781, they were married.[9]

Although Mary was past the age of forty and John Fletcher was ten years older, they sought Wesley's approval before they announced their wedding plans. This was the standard procedure in Methodist circles. Wesley "approved it entirely, being persuaded it would be much to the glory of God."[10]

The wedding ceremony itself was short, but afterward they returned home with close friends and continued the conversation in the spirit of that solemn ceremony. A friend presented them with some wedding hymns, and Fletcher read the Scripture printed on the top of one of them: "Husbands, love your wives," to which he added, "as Christ loved the Church." His comments were poignant: "My God, what a task! Help me, my friends, by your prayers to fulfil it. As Christ loved the Church! He laid aside his glory for her! . . . O my God, none is able to fulfil this task without thine almighty aid." He then read the next text: "Wives, submit yourselves unto your own husbands," and Mary added, "as unto the Lord." Again Fletcher added his own commentary: "Well, my dear, only in the Lord. And if ever I wish you to do any thing otherwise, resist me with all your might."[11]

Although Mary and John Fletcher were no doubt set in their ways after so many years of independent living, they apparently adjusted to married life quickly. Their maturity and their mutual commitment to ministry gave them a basis for a happy and fulfilling partnership. They also shared an uncommon love for children. They would never have any of their own, but they both gave sacrificially to the care and ministry of children. Before their marriage Fletcher had organized a school for poor children in his parish, and he established a Sunday school that grew to more than three hundred.[12]

It was these common interests and concerns that helped bind them together in love. Not long after they were married, Mary wrote in her journal of her deep contentment:

> I have such a husband as is in everything suited to me. He bears with all my faults and failings, in a manner which continually reminds me of that word, "Love your wives as Christ loved the Church." His constant endeavor is to make me happy; his strongest desire, my spiritual growth. He is in every sense of the word, the man my highest reason chooses to obey.[13]

On another occasion Mary wrote, "I have the best of husbands, who daily grows more and more spiritual, and I think more healthful, being far better than when we first married. My call is also so clear, and I have such liberty in the work, and such sweet encouragement among the people."[14]

Fletcher was initially more hesitant in speaking of the marital bliss they were experiencing—perhaps fearing that once the "honeymoon" was over, the marriage would turn sour. "I was afraid at first to say much of the matter," he wrote to a friend, "for new-married people do not, at first, know each other; but having now lived fourteen months in my new state, I can tell you, Providence has reserved a *prize* for me, and that my wife is far better to me than the church to Christ; so that if the parallel fail, it will be on my side."[15]

Mary eagerly joined her husband in parish ministry and was entirely happy as a pastor's wife. "In the years of their residence at Madeley," writes Earl Kent Brown, "the Fletchers pursued what can only be seen as a joint ministry. They were partners, not master and servant." She shared in his visitation duties, met with

Methodist classes and bands, and "spoke regularly in the several preaching places in the large parish as well as out of doors. . . . She also entertained a steady stream of itinerating ministers."[16]

Preaching was not new to Mary. Before she married Fletcher, she had been an itinerant preacher at the same time she was directing the orphanage. She was convinced that this was the ministry God had for her, but she was also very aware of the potential for criticism. So she took every precaution to accommodate those who might object to a woman in a leadership role. It was her "custom to do her speaking from the steps leading to the pulpit in the society chapels rather than proceeding to the pulpit itself." Another concession that she granted her listeners related to her precise style of preaching, as she herself testified in a letter: "For some years I was often led to speak from a text. Of late I feel greater approbation in what we call *expounding,* taking a part or whole of a chapter and speaking on it."[17] Apparently some of her listeners regarded speaking "from a text" too close to sermonizing, but "expounding" was simply giving commentary on God's Word.

Mary saw great success in her ministry. On one occasion after she preached, a Mr. Varty accompanied her home to talk further about his spiritual state. Through her counsel he was converted, and soon after that he started a society and built a chapel in his hometown.[18]

Wesley was initially very opposed to the concept of women preaching, but when he realized the value of their contributions, his convictions slowly began to change. In 1771, a decade before she married Fletcher, Wesley wrote to Mary to affirm her in her work: "I think the strength of the cause rests there—on your having an *extraordinary* call." He went on to argue that "the whole work of God termed Methodism is an extraordinary dispensation," and therefore it did "not fall under the ordinary rules of discipline." Thus Paul's injunction against women speaking did not absolutely apply.[19]

Fletcher, too, encouraged Mary in her preaching, and when they traveled to Ireland to do Methodist itinerant work, "both preached; both led classes and bands; both made endless cultivation calls." They were an effective team as the 100-percent increase in the Dublin Society during their ministry there would indicate. In 1784 they traveled to Yorkshire and conducted a similar tour of service, and again they had remarkable success.[20]

Shortly after they were married, Charles Wesley had written a letter to Fletcher in which he related his happiness over their union: "Yours, I believe, is one of the few marriages that is made in heaven." And it truly seemed to be—for that short period of "three years, nine months, and two days." Fletcher was not a well man when Mary married him, and thus to some it was not shocking news when they heard that at age fifty-five he had died of tuberculosis—what was described as "consumptive complaint."[21]

Mary was devastated. Having waited so long to be married, finding God's perfect choice, and then being left a widow at forty-five was almost too much to bear. To a friend she wrote, "It seems to me I both *love and miss him* every day *more and more.*" She was tempted to give up, but she plodded on in ministry despite her intense grief. She had no choice. When he married her, Fletcher had chided her that "when you marry me, you must marry my parish." She took those words seriously, and though he was gone, that part of the marriage remained. The ministry had to go forward. Yet it was not without pain. Three years after his death she wrote, "Never did I know three years of such suffering, and never did I know three years of such prayer."[22]

John Wesley advised Mary to move to London after Fletcher's death, believing that her ministry would be most useful there. But she was more inclined to stay. That is what her husband had requested on his deathbed. The new vicar resided outside the parish, and thus Mary was able to remain in the parsonage. Because of the vicar's nonresidence, Mary continued to serve the parish much as she had done while her husband was alive. She wrote that it provided her immense opportunities for service: "I was never in any situation in which I had so much opportunity of doing good . . . as in this place and that in various ways, public and private."[23]

One of her greatest contributions to the work in the Madeley parish was her ability to bring unity among the Methodists and Anglicans. "Church folk and the Methodists," according to Earl Kent Brown, "continued to blend into one fellowship during those troubled years when most Methodists elsewhere in England felt forced out of the established churches. Mrs. Fletcher was the 'mystery ingredient' that made the mixture work in Madeley. It did not last long after her death."[24]

In addition to counseling and charitable work, Mary continued to preach after Fletcher's death, "at times to crowds as large as three thousand. Clergymen were regularly seen in her congregation, thus making her a 'minister to ministers.' "[25] Because of the opposition to women in the pulpit, she did not preach in formal Anglican services, but rather confined her preaching to the "tythe barn," located near the parish house where she lived. It was an old building that had been designated for lay Methodist preachers who frequently passed through the parish; but she was unofficially the "pastor," and under her direction the building was almost constantly in use.

> In the years following Mr. Fletcher's death, this room became her special place. The Methodists met first on Sunday a.m. before regular church services. She would pray first and then speak for fifteen minutes or so on the "Watchword" of the day. Then she invited visitors present to express their experience, with occasional cautions and interjections from herself. Then regular attendants might testify, with her comments following. When the church bell tolled, they adjourned to the parish church. At noon, the visitors ate with her, and at 1:00 the meeting resumed. She read portions of the life of some eminent Christian and added extensive comments. They adjourned for the afternoon parish church service, but at 7:00 would be back in the "tythe barn," or in one of the nearby chapels. There, the evening service would be led by an itinerant if one were present, or by Mrs. Fletcher otherwise. During the week, there were meetings on from two to five of the nights. Here, she generally expounded some passage from scripture. . . . It was not uncommon for the Anglican curate and other nearby parish priests to attend these services.[26]

Because of her noncombative style and her obvious spiritual maturity, Mary was generally not perceived as a threat by the men with whom she worked so closely. There were occasions, however, when the issue of her sex arose—when men simply could not accept her public preaching ministry. In such instances, she usually let others settle the issue (such as John Wesley), without becoming involved in the fray itself, or she simply trusted God to resolve the matter.

One example of the latter is the case of "Mr. G." When Mr. G heard that Mary was scheduled to speak, he sought to change her mind. He told her he would speak in her place, and when that did not dissuade her, he proceeded to the pulpit without her approval. But he had hardly opened his mouth to speak, when the words stopped. His mind went blank. "It appears God shut his mouth," wrote an early Methodist leader, "for he could say no more. He came down and never opposed her afterwards."[27]

There were other occasions when Mary faced opposition and was provoked into defending her ministry, though sometimes she understood why some might object to it. "I know the power of God," she wrote, "which I have felt when standing on the horse-block in the street at Huddersfield; but at the same time I am conscious how ridiculous I must appear in the eyes of many for so doing. Therefore, if some persons consider me as an impudent woman, and represent me as such, I cannot blame them."

Some of Mary's critics suggested that her "call" was a "Quaker call," because Quakers encouraged women to preach, and they told her, "You are an offence to us; go to the people whose call is the same as your own . . . : here nobody can bear with you." To that Mary responded, "Though I believe the Quakers have still a good deal of God among them, yet I think the Spirit of the Lord is more at work among the Methodists; and . . . though they were to toss me about as a foot-ball, I would stick to them like a leech. Besides, I do nothing but what Mr. Wesley approves."[28]

"Widow Fletcher," as she was known to many, continued an active ministry for more than a quarter of a century after her husband's death. When friends visited her at the age of seventy, they found her still involved in a half-dozen meetings each week and doing the main preaching in two of those meetings. She found deep peace during those later years, no longer suffering the searing pain of her husband's death. She had apparently soothed her sorrow through a sense of mystical communion with her late husband. Soon after his passing, she had written a tract entitled "Thoughts on Communion," in which she dealt with that possibility that he was still in a sense present with her. Such thoughts were a healing balm as her journal in 1790 indicates: "My house is a sweet rest, and a 'secret place in the wilderness to hide me in'. . . .

I have peace within. . . . I have communion with my friends above."[29]

Mary's active ministry continued until the year of her death in 1815, when she was seventy-six. She preached her final sermon in the summer of that year and continued to work with class meetings into the fall. She died in December.[30] She has since been eulogized as one of the most outstanding women in early Methodism. Her many years of Methodist society and children's ministry were highly praised by John Wesley, but even more noteworthy were her thirty-four years of powerful ministry as a pastor's wife—thirty years of which she served as a widow.

SARAH EDWARDS

• 6 •
Sarah Edwards
Reaping the Rancor
of Petty Complaints

Perhaps no one in the congregation is subjected to more stringent criticism than the pastor's wife," writes Lora Lee Parrott. "She may be criticized for what she has done, or what she has not done, or what she could have done. Not only is she criticized for what she does but for what her husband does, or her children. She will be criticized if she assists her husband too much in the parish work, or criticized if she does not do enough."[1]

It often seems that no matter what a pastor's wife does, people are watching and ready to complain. According to Parrott, there are two basic reasons for this. The first is that she "moves in semi-limelight" and "is constantly on the spot." Her "choice of dress, her make-up or lack of it, her public care of the children, her social graces or inabilities are paraded before all interested eyes." The second is even more difficult to cope with: "laymen have a standard of perfection for the pastor's wife." In their eyes, she must "be neat, wise, happy, frugal, deft, strong, feminine," and "spiritual." Parrott argues that "such a standard of perfection is not even held for the pastor himself."[2]

The title of Denise Turner's book—*Home Sweet Fishbowl*—captures this common complaint of pastors' wives. They live in a fishbowl—some call it a house of glass—and often resent "being watched, pressured, and criticized" by the parishioners who perceive it their duty to guard the pedestal position of the pastor's wife. Often people in the parish have a stereotypical image of how the pastor's wife should look and act. "The fact is," writes Turner, "that a number of people do expect their minister's wife to look a certain way. That certain way, although it is never actually spelled out, is probably best described as inexpensively presentable—sort of early sweetly dowdy, bargain basement style."[3]

Likewise, "many people expect a minister's wife to be a great cook too—not the elaborate ingredients and lavish dishes kind of cook, but the kind of cook who can turn out pure country gourmet on a shoestring."[4] Living on a shoestring is a reality for many pastors' wives. It is true that the problem is not unique to the profession, but pastors' wives face a unique set of circumstances by having their income controlled by church board members, many of whom inwardly, if not outwardly, begrudge any hint of extravagance that might surface in the pastor's family.

Sarah Edwards, like Idelette Calvin, was a pastor's wife in a very conservative, traditional sense—if the traditional role is being a supportive, behind-the-scenes partner in the ministry. Like many pastors' wives before and after her, Sarah found fulfillment in her husband's ministry and was not inclined to stake out a ministry in her own right as Katherine Zell had done. This, some might argue, would certainly be a safe turf for a woman who wishes to avoid controversy. If a pastor's wife models the Christian life without taking strong positions or eclipsing her husband, she will be free from the criticism and backbiting that her more outspoken sisters confront. Not so. As most pastors' wives in that situation know, their struggles are often as great as if they were center stage themselves. The life and ministry of Sarah Edwards, the wife of Jonathan Edwards—one of America's greatest theologians and preachers—aptly illustrate this.

Sarah was a young bride. She was seventeen and he was twenty-four. She had first met Edwards when she was thirteen, and in that year he wrote his perceptions of her. It was her spiritual maturity that impressed him the most. He wrote that God "comes to her and fills her mind with exceeding sweet delight, and that she hardly cares for anything, except to meditate on him. . . . She is of a wonderful sweetness, calmness and universal benevolence of mind; especially after this Great God has manifested himself to her mind." In his view, her outward manner matched her inner depth: "She will sometimes go about from place to place, singing sweetly; and seems to be always full of joy and pleasure; . . . she loves to be alone, walking in the fields and groves, and seems to have some one invisible always conversing with her."[5]

In many ways Jonathan and Sarah were an unmatched pair. "It is remarkable that these two survived their courtship," writes Elizabeth Dodds. "Moody, socially bumbling, barricaded behind the stateliness of the very shy, Edwards was totally unlike the girl who fatefully caught his eye. She was a vibrant brunette, with erect posture and burnished manners. She was skillful at small talk—he had no talent for it at all. She was blithe—he given to black patches of introspection."[6]

Yet their personalities complemented each other's in a way that allowed for an effective partnership that lasted all their married life. They had a shared ministry, and they shared the struggles that were so prevalent during their years of service together. They had a close and tender relationship, and this helped them endure trying ordeals. Edwards's love for his wife was extraordinary, but perhaps not unusual, considering his Puritan heritage. According to Amanda Porterfield, "One of the most striking phenomena about the New England Puritans is that their greatest ministers . . . loved their wives beyond measure."[7]

Sarah's initiation into the role of pastor's wife was met with high expectations. Her husband was called to the Congregational church in Northampton, Massachusetts, to serve as an assistant to his grandfather. Solomon Stoddard—no ordinary pastor—was eighty-five and had not missed a scheduled sermon in fifty-seven years at the church. He was revered by his six hundred parishioners, and filling his shoes was no easy task for Edwards.

Though the church had been without a pastor's wife for some time, Sarah was well aware of the demands that would be placed on her in the months and years to follow. Indeed, the churches in Colonial New England virtually enshrined their pastors' wives with the expectation that they would exhibit the saintliness that deserved such reverence.

On her first Sunday in Northampton, Sarah "took her place in the seat that was to symbolize her role—a high bench facing the congregation, where everyone could notice the least flicker of expression." Although since childhood she was familiar with this practice, it nevertheless must have been unnerving to know that every eye was focused on her. "Other women could yawn or furtively twitch a numbed foot in the cold of a January morning in an unheated building. Never she. Others could have weekday lapses—snarl at stupid tradesmen or admit to simple fatigue—but when the minister's wife showed human frailties, it was the subject of conversation."[8]

But Sarah's good qualities were also the subject of conversation. She quickly established a reputation as a good mother. According to her husband, "She thought that, as a parent, she had great and important duties to do towards her children, before they were capable of government and instruction. For them, she constantly and earnestly prayed." She also "regularly prayed with her children." Whether she actually "never had to speak but once" and "was cheerfully obeyed," as her husband's early biographer contends, is open to question, but she was viewed as a loving and highly capable mother and a good disciplinarian.[9]

Likewise, Sarah was known for her spiritual care of others. Dr. Samuel Hopkins, who knew her well, wrote, "She was eminent for her piety, and for experimental religion. Religious conversation was her delight; and, as far as propriety permitted she promoted it in all companies." She was also a pioneer in the matter of women's ministries.

> She always prized highly the privilege of social worship, not only in the family, but in the private meetings of Christians. Such meetings, on the part of females *only,* for prayer and religious conversation, have at times been objected to, as, both in their nature and results, inconsistent with the true delicacy of the sex. Her own judgment, formed deliberately, and in coincidence with that of her husband, was in favour of these meetings; and accordingly, she regularly encouraged and promoted them . . . attending on them herself, and not declining to take her proper share in the performance of their various duties. In this way, she exerted an important influence among her own sex.[10]

But despite her reputation for spiritual leadership, Sarah would discover that even the most innocent of circumstances involving her marriage and family, when whispered from one parishioner to another, had the potential for scandal and gossip. That Sarah and Jonathan had a strong and loving relationship was not questioned, but how and when they expressed their love apparently was. It was widely believed in Colonial New England that a baby was born on the same day of the week that it had been conceived, and some ministers actually refused to baptize babies born on Sunday and thus conceived in sin. Sexual intimacy was not deemed an appropriate activity on the Sabbath, particularly for a minister. It did not go without notice, therefore, that six of their eleven children were conspicuously born on Sunday.[11]

In many other ways Sarah must have often felt as though she lived in a glass house. There was the issue of salary—not an uncommon problem that arises between pastor and congregation. Many ministers of the day received substantial gifts in addition to their yearly salary, but Edwards—who was often at odds with members of his congregation—was seldom the recipient of private donations of this kind. The increasing expenses required to maintain a growing family prompted Edwards to disclose his needs to the town officials. A committee was set up to deal with the issue, but instead of a quick decision, the matter was left unsettled, with Sarah being asked to keep an itemized account of all expenses.[12]

The request for itemization exposed the underlying suspicion of many parishioners that Sarah was too extravagant in her tastes. The suspicions were not entirely unfounded. She had not hesitated to wear an expensive brooch that her husband had given her from his outside earnings on his writing, and she clearly had a flair for home decorating and fashion design. She also had an uncanny ability to visually appropriate ideas from a Boston dress shop and return to Northampton and duplicate the styles—sometimes by remaking old clothes. The result was that she and her daughters had more stylish clothes than most of the other women in the congregation.[13]

Did Sarah have too much of a flair for fashion? Should a pastor's wife be cautious in her dress in order to avoid criticism? Should she seek to follow the norm in dress and fashion? Pastors' wives during this era were expected to abide by an accepted standard. "A modest simplicity became the norm. Costly jewelry and gaudy frills were forbidden. The wife of a minister ought to so dress that the poor would feel welcome in church, the reasoning went. The money that went to purchase that piece of jewelry might have better gone to send tracts to China."[14] These were difficult issues for pastors' wives of prior generations, and they still confront pastors' wives today.

As a pastor's wife, Sarah found that it was more than outward issues like fashion that became an issue among parishioners. In spiritual matters as well, she was not to carry things to an extreme. She discovered this in 1742, during a period of revival when her husband was away preaching. She later related how she wept for long periods of time and was "filled with such intense admiration of the wonderful condescension and grace of God" that she lost all her "bodily strength." After that, she relates, "I could with difficulty refrain from rising from my seat, and leaping for joy. I continued to enjoy this intense, and lively and refreshing sense of Divine things, accompanied with strong emotions, for nearly an hour, after which, I experienced a delightful calm."[15]

This was not a modern Pentecostal or charismatic meeting. It was strait-laced Congregational Puritanism, and in the minds of many, the pastor's wife was making an unnecessary spectacle of herself. "It appears," writes Ola Elizabeth Winslow, "that she was the central figure in the meetinghouse drama, and that her bodily state under stress of her ecstasies was such as to cause alarm to some of her neighbors, who feared that the 'effect might be fatal before Mr. Edwards' return.'"[16]

One of the enduring struggles Sarah faced as a pastor's wife from the very earliest years of her ministry was that of sharing her husband with other women. Then as now, there were many more women than men actively involved in the churches. Some of these women were widowed or had never married, and others were married to unbelievers. For them, their pastor was often the only man they could relate to spiritually, and some may have vicariously identified with him as the husband they so longed for. Sarah was pleased that women revered her husband and depended on him as a spiritual leader, but there was always a concern that such feelings not be carried too far; for Sarah, it was just one more adjustment to life in the parsonage.[17]

But if Sarah sometimes felt uncomfortable because her

husband was receiving too much admiration and attention, there were other times when she felt just the opposite. One such occasion came during the previously mentioned revival in the winter of 1742, after she and her husband had been in the ministry some fifteen years. Edwards was out of town, and the pulpit was being filled by Mr. Buell, a young personable evangelist who quickly won the hearts of the parishioners. Sarah reacted as most pastors' wives would. Of course she wanted God to work through this visiting speaker, but deep down she desperately did not want him to upstage her husband. She was aware of her feelings, and her personal reflections indicate her honesty and spiritual depth.

> I heard that Mr. Buell was coming to this town, and from what I had heard of him and of his success, I had strong hopes that there would be great effects from his labors here. At the same time . . . it greatly concerned me to watch my heart and see to it that I was perfectly resigned to God, with respect to the instruments he should make use of to revive religion in this town, and be entirely willing, if it was God's pleasure, that he should make use of Mr. Buell.[18]

The struggle that Sarah endured was compounded by the obvious fact that her husband was not altogether popular among the townspeople who supported him with their tax dollars and who considered him their pastor, whether they frequented church regularly or not. Jonathan Edwards was a man of strong conviction, and he refused to compromise his stand on issues to gain the support of his parishioners. His campaign against taverns infuriated many of those whose social life was centered about the local saloon. Edwards himself was too busy with sermon preparation and writing to socialize. He was perceived as being too scholarly and uninterested in the mundane concerns of his people.

In some instances Edwards dealt with problems in a high-handed manner without the sensitivity that was desperately needed. That was true in 1744, when rumors surfaced that some of the teenagers in the church were secretly reading a midwives' instruction manual and passing it on to their friends. To Edwards this was a shocking state of affairs, and he felt it was his responsibility to get to the bottom of the matter immediately. After a hasty investigation, he announced on Sunday morning those who should appear for further questioning, without distinguishing between those who were believed guilty and those who had reported them. It created an uproar in the church and community, and he later confessed that he might have more properly handled the affair by going to the individuals privately.[19]

Edwards could rightly be faulted on his inability to approach his parishioners on their level, and in some instances that inability hindered his efforts to persuade them to follow the proper course in church matters. Such was the case in 1749 when his opposition to the Half-Way Covenant created bitter controversy in the church. The Half-Way Covenant allowed individuals who had not had a conversion experience to become members of the church and to have their children baptized. Edwards's own grandfather, Solomon Stoddard, had helped to formulate this policy, so it is not surprising that there would be powerful objections to any effort to reverse the trend and require stricter standards for membership.

It was this issue that caused the greatest anguish during their long ministry in Northampton, and as is typically the case, Sarah, as the pastor's wife, probably suffered far more than her husband. "Church was a hollow ordeal for pastor and people. Edwards continued to work over his sermons until they were burnished brilliantly. Sarah, watching the stony faces in the pew, knew that few people were listening receptively."[20]

Church attendance decreased, and between 1744 and 1748 no new applications for membership were received. The ordeal finally came to a climax in 1750, when two hundred church members signed a petition to remove Edwards from the pulpit. The matter was taken to the Hampshire Association of Churches, where Edwards was judged by fellow ministers and in a vote of eight to seven was dismissed from his parish of twenty-three years. On July 2, 1750, he preached his farewell sermon, but because he had no place to go and the church had no pastor, he served as a substitute in his own pulpit. It was a humiliating ordeal, but the alternative was no ministry at all. A friend offered to help them financially if Edwards would stay and minister to the families who had supported him, but he was loath to split the church.[21]

After some months in limbo, Edwards received a call to be a missionary to the Indians in the frontier settlement of Stock-bridge. In the eyes of many it was no doubt viewed as an embarrassing demotion, but Sarah and Jonathan regarded it as the will of the Lord and an opportunity for further ministry. Rather than sulking and being bitter, Sarah, according to Jonathan, thrived in the new environment: "My wife and children are well-pleased with our present situation. They like the place much better than they expected. Here, at present, we live in peace; which has of long time been an unusual thing with us. The Indians seem much pleased with my family, especially my wife."[22]

After several years of ministry in Stockbridge, during which time he continued his scholarly writing, Edwards was invited to assume the presidency of Princeton. It was a tough decision for him and Sarah to make, but in the February chill of 1758 he left for New Jersey, with plans for Sarah to follow later in the spring. Five weeks later, however, he was dead. Fearing the effects of a smallpox epidemic, Edwards had agreed to be inoculated—a procedure still in its experimental stages. It was a fateful decision—one that plunged Sarah suddenly into the deepest crisis of her life. Several weeks later, her sorrow was compounded when her married daughter Esther also died of the inoculation, leaving her children for Sarah to care for. The emotional pain and added burdens, however, were too much for Sarah to endure. She died later that same year.

Sarah Edwards had made every effort to be the truly effective first lady of a New England meetinghouse. But she lived in an era when little leeway was given for different lifestyles, mistakes in judgment, or atypical behavior. On many occasions Sarah ignored community censure, convinced that she had God's blessing and the trust of her husband. In fact, it was a deep mutual trust and commitment that propelled them through many crises. When Sarah was experiencing spiritual ecstasies that might have embarrassed any other theological heavyweight, Jonathan Edwards, who had previously feared the consequences of such emotional outbursts, accepted her experience as being from God and later asked her to write down her testimony that it might be preserved. When others let them down, Sarah and Jonathan knew they could count on each other, and that factor more than anything else brought them through the crises they confronted in pastoral ministry.

EUNICE BEECHER

• 7 •
Eunice Beecher
Struggling With the
Scandal of the Century

News wires in April carried the story of a California pastor who was confronted by church authorities for alleged impropriety with a married woman he was counseling."

This was the opening paragraph of an article entitled "Let's Let Women Counsel Women" that appeared in *Moody Monthly* in 1980. The major premise of the article is summed up in one terse paragraph: "The problem is obvious. Pastors are men. Their counselees are often women in distress. A relationship develops. It is discovered. The roof caves in." According to the authors, "Pastors have no business counseling women." Their advice: "There is a vast army of godly women who could help pastors and help turn the tide of broken homes that is sweeping into the evangelical church."[1]

Even when infidelity is not an issue in the pastoral counseling of women, it can cause problems in the pastor's relationship with his wife and children. "It's difficult for a wife to observe her husband's patience with others," writes Frances Nordland, "and then fail to see the same patience exercised in his dealing with her and their children. A pastor who spends an hour patiently listening to someone's problem may become very curt with his wife when she presents to him problems that to him seem petty." But a more serious problem, as Nordland perceives it, is when pastors are involved in intimate counseling with women. She tells of the results of this for one pastor: "His unfaithfulness started as a result of counseling *alone* those persons who should have been counseled only with another lady present. We definitely feel that it is very important for the pastor and his wife to counsel as a team those who ask for counsel who are of the opposite sex."[2]

Eunice Beecher might have wished many times that her husband had taken such advice before he began counseling Libby Tilton. A close relationship developed apparently only after what had initially been an innocent effort made by a pastor to counsel a parishioner who was encountering marital stress. For Eunice, it was a traumatic ordeal that was probably compounded by the fact that she was married to one of the most famous American preachers of all time.

Henry Ward Beecher served as the pastor of the large and prestigious Plymouth Church of Brooklyn (Congregational) for forty years. He was the son of the renowned Lyman Beecher and the brother of Harriet Beecher Stowe, who would become famous for her book *Uncle Tom's Cabin.* Henry was widely known for his political activism, and he had an illustrious reputation for witty and dynamic sermons. Eunice, unlike her husband, did not draw attention and adulation. She was primarily concerned with her family, and she generally stood in the shadow of her larger-than-life husband.

Eunice was the daughter of Dr. Artemas Bullard of West Sutton, Massachusetts. She first met Beecher in 1831, when, as a student at Amherst College, he and another student came home with her brother on term break. She liked him immediately and later recalled "the roguish mouth, the laughing, merry eyes, the quaint humor and quick repartee."

Yet there was initially no thought of romance for Eunice. She wrote, "Truth to tell, [he was] an exceedingly homely young man." His attraction for her was no less unspectacular. She later wrote of their earliest times together: "Mother and I were necessarily much of the time busy in the kitchen, milk-cellar, dairy, etc., but these young collegians found those places most attractive. The gentle way mother smiled at all the younger one's mischievous pranks was a source of perpetual delight to him. He always said he fell in love with my mother, and, not being able to get her, took up with me."[3]

Several months after this first meeting, Eunice, who was trained as a schoolteacher, renewed her acquaintance with Beecher, who gladly accepted her father's suggestion that he tutor her in Latin. She was a bit taken aback by the suggestion. "Even though he was now a Sophomore, I didn't believe he could help me much—*I* who had been a school-ma'am for three terms!"[4]

Beecher wasted no time in getting to the heart of his mission in the tutoring assignment. After asking Eunice to conjugate the verb *amo,* she wrote, "he slipped a bit of paper on to my writing-desk: 'Will you go with me as missionary to the West?'" Eunice did not readily agree, nor did her parents, who believed the couple were much too young. But within a few months their engagement was made official with an engagement ring—in the words of Eunice, "a plain gold ring, which was also my wedding-ring." It was certainly not a storybook romance. Beecher bought the ring out of a ten-dollar honorarium he had received for a lecture, with enough money remaining to purchase books.[5]

It was a long engagement. After graduating from Amherst, Beecher studied at Lane Seminary in Cincinnati, after which he served in two tiny parishes. "For seven years, like Jacob of old, he had labored, waiting for the time when he could claim his wife. Of course, until he was settled somewhere with some definite income, it was folly to think of marrying."[6]

There may have been other factors that cooled Henry's desire to hurry into matrimony with Eunice. According to Paxton Hibben, "In the three years he spent at Lane at least three young ladies held him enthralled." To one he wrote romantic love letters, but to Eunice, "theology predominated in his letters." Any romance that was lacking in letters was hardly made up for in person. In the four years that he was in the Midwest prior to his return for their marriage, they had been together only two days.[7]

Despite the long engagement, the wedding came suddenly. Beecher was serving in a small parish in Lawrenceburg, Indiana, and in the summer of 1837 he wrote to Eunice suggesting that they marry in September after his ordination. But he soon changed his mind and sent a second letter, telling her he would be returning immediately for the wedding. Both he and the letter, to the surprise of Eunice and her family, arrived on July 29, and the wedding took place five days later.[8]

By the end of August the newlyweds were getting settled in Lawrenceburg, a town of less than three thousand residents. Beecher's meager salary was not enough for them to set up housekeeping on their own, so "he accepted the hospitality of one of his elders, who had offered him a room in his house." When their welcome there was exhausted, they rented two rooms above a barn at the rate of forty dollars a year. With the help of friends who donated household items, and with the sale of her "cloak" for thirty dollars, Eunice was able to turn the dingy surroundings into "quite a pleasant home."[9]

In later life, when she reflected back on these early days on the frontier, Eunice was almost nostalgic. But at the time, this "strait-laced . . . New England girl" found it very difficult to adjust. "What is certain," according to Hibben, "is that Eunice Beecher hated the life in Indiana with a bitterness that grew fiercer every year." The parishioners were "a hard-headed, horny-handed, close-fisted lot who . . . had little patience with the wails of a twenty-five-year-old bride who regretted that she could not afford a servant and felt put upon to have to do sewing or take in boarders to piece out her husband's income."[10]

In 1839, Beecher received a call from a congregation of thirty in Indianapolis. It was a step up from his tiny parish in Lawrenceburg, and he accepted. Eunice found the new environment no more to her liking than the old, and the parishioners were not sure what to make of her. One woman wrote, "I had never seen such a woman: she could be as beautiful as a princess, and as plain and homely as possible. So she could be sparklingly bright and bitterly sarcastic." Beecher was also criticized, but despite the limitations, it was in Indianapolis that his ministry blossomed. His tiny church grew to nearly three hundred members, and a new church building was erected.[11]

After eight years in Indianapolis, Beecher accepted a call to Plymouth Church in Brooklyn, New York, and in 1847 he was installed as the pastor. For Eunice, it was a welcome change. It meant a much higher standard of living and a cultural environment more suited to her. But life was still not easy, as Paxton Hibben relates: "Poor Eunice lost another baby shortly after her arrival and was due to have her sixth child in January. Life was literally just one baby after another for Eunice Beecher."[12]

There were other problems for Eunice also. Although she was able to hire servants to relieve her of many domestic responsibilities, she felt a loneliness that she had not experienced in the Midwest, and she looked back at those days with a sense of loss. "With all these discomforts, I had a far more thorough knowledge of Mr. Beecher's inner life, his thoughts and feelings," she wrote, "than I ever had after we came East." In New York her relationship with him suddenly began to change. "When I got here to Brooklyn the public began to take my husband away from me. His study was no longer in the house but in the church. And when he went out, I used to gasp for breath, and my eyes would fill with tears, for it seemed to me as if we had quarreled."[13]

Beecher himself alluded to these marital problems when he contrasted his personality with his wife's:

> Domestic unhappiness comes from the fact that people do not know or do not enough recognize the peculiarities of each other's natures. They expect impossible things of each other. If a flaming, demonstrative nature and a cool, undemonstrative nature come together, neither of whom understands or makes allowance for the peculiarities of the other, there can hardly fail to be unhappiness.[14]

Henry's letters to Eunice during his New York years indicate that they had grown distant in their relationship. They "became more impersonal and perfunctory."[15]

Eunice had much in her life that brought unhappiness during her husband's four decades of ministry in New York, but she carved out a writing ministry for herself that helped her overcome the painful loss of four of her nine children and the grief associated with her marital trials. In 1859 she published a novel, *From Dawn to Daylight: The Simple Story of a Western Home*. She wrote many articles on motherhood and the home for religious and secular publications. In the novel she presents a very traditional view of male headship in the home, but she challenges the husband to be sensitive to his wife: "Will he deal gently with her always—remembering that he is now her all—that for his dear sake, she leaves every tie, and each familiar scene, to follow him into a land of strangers?"[16]

Philosophical issues came between the Beechers also. Henry was a political activist who had taken a strong stand against slavery. Eunice accepted his public pronouncements on that issue, but when he began speaking for the cause of women's suffrage, she was distressed. "I have no sympathy for the new woman," she wrote. "What is the ability to speak on a public platform or the wisdom that may command a seat on a judge's bench compared to that which can insure and preside over a true home?" She claimed that the female supporters of suffrage "ignored the sweeter, more delicate and feminine home duties for the rougher, coarser duties that were ordained to be man's special work."[17]

Like many women, however, Eunice herself did not necessarily follow the traditional course she outlined for women. She became a lyceum lecturer for a short time in the 1860s, reading and interpreting her husband's lectures. After her first effort, her husband rebuked her for claiming he believed "God was black, that Christ was a Mulatto, that the Devil was white," and that he wished he had been born black himself. He wrote, "Now my dear, you must allow me to protest against your lecturing if such sentiments are to be propounded."[18]

In theory Eunice had definite ideas about the proper role and duties for a wife, as she described them in *From Dawn to Daylight:*

> . . . to place a higher estimate on purely domestic qualifications—to feel that a woman's proper ambition should be the endeavor to relieve her husband . . . from those homecares which are incompatible with high mental effort—that he may turn, when wearied and perplexed with parochial or public duties, to his own hearth as a *resting place*—the sweetest earthly refuge from care and trouble.[19]

Like most women of her day, she truly believed that women's suffrage would undermine family life. She was a sentimentalist of sorts in her perception of the home: "All pure love, all right thoughts, all religion, if you would have them live, must have their roots beneath the altar of the home." She took her role as homemaker and her task of child rearing very seriously and was a strict disciplinarian. She brought up the children to reverence their parents, not permitting them such familiarities as saying "Hello, mamma!" or "Hello, papa!" or other endearments that she regarded improper. These rules for family living were not simply a private matter. For a time in the 1870s she wrote a column, "Motherly Talks," in her husband's weekly religious journal.[20]

It is not surprising, then, that Eunice would resent her husband's involvement in the women's suffrage movement and his association with such women as Susan B. Anthony and Elizabeth Cady Stanton. To her they were the epitome of that brand of female who was seeking to revolutionize family life by giving women the franchise. But there were other aspects of her husband's association with women that distressed her even more. One of Beecher's close associates characterized Eunice as "one of the most jealous women that ever lived" and described Henry's domestic life as "hell upon earth." Whatever the validity of that judgment, there was no doubt justification for some of Eunice's suspicions and indignation. Rumors about her husband's attentions to other women had surfaced even before they had left Indianapolis, and there were more rumors during his years in Brooklyn.[21]

It would be expected that a prominent minister could not continue in such questionable activities with certain of his female parishioners indefinitely without a scandal, and Beecher was no exception. He was a middle-aged man at the peak of his career when the bubble burst. Elizabeth Tilton was the woman in question—a young mother who was twenty-two years younger than he. She was a Sunday school teacher at Plymouth Church, and she also conducted classes for poor women. Her husband had been a close associate and loyal friend, and Beecher spent a great deal of time in their home.

"Libby" was a good listener and an admiring critic of Beecher's writing, and she soon became his closest confidante. When her husband was away on lecture tours for months at a time, Libby could count on her pastor to visit her and express his concern for the trials she was enduring. According to Beecher, she "gave an account of what she had seen of cruelty and abuse on the part of the husband that shocked me." It was in that context that the alleged sexual misconduct occurred.[22]

The improprieties first began to surface when Libby felt constrained to confess to her husband. Furious with his pastor, Tilton told others, and the rumors began to fly. When confronted by the charges, Beecher admitted that he had taken liberties with Libby, but he insisted that it only amounted to kissing. He claimed that she was the one who sought him out for consolation and security in the midst of marital difficulties—though he praised her innocence and was careful not to place any blame on her. He did not hesitate, however, to implicate Theodore Tilton, Libby's husband, in sexual misconduct of his own, and Eunice joined those who sought to blacken Tilton's reputation. The scandal smoldered beneath the surface for more than a year, while an intermediary outside the church family sought to reconcile Beecher with the Tiltons and others who had become involved.

In the late spring of 1871, the story broke publicly, and it was then that the scandal began to have its effect on Eunice. "She is white-haired," wrote an acquaintance, "and looks a dozen years older than when I last had a near view of her. My heart has been full of pity for her. . . . Her face is written over with many volumes of human suffering."

Outwardly Eunice defended her husband's innocence, as she later related in his biography, and she held no visible animosity toward Libby Tilton. Libby herself had endured painful humiliation, but her love and loyalty for her pastor did not waver. "I have had sorrow almost beyond human capacity," she confided to a friend. "We have weathered the storm, and, I believe, without harm to our *Best*"—referring to Henry. This, however, was written before the scandal broke in the newspapers.[23]

During most of this period, Eunice was deliberately excluded from the negotiations and developments. Henry kept personal papers at his sister's home and spent as much time as he could away from his own home. Eunice vacationed in Florida and Havana. From there she wrote to him, apparently believing his innocence but unaware of many of the accusations that were being hurled at him. In 1872 Henry wrote to her, "Thanks for your letter from Jacksonville. It cheered me. God knows that I do not need any more loads; and a comforting letter never could come to a better market." He went on to appeal to her sympathies, lamenting that "my life is almost over." In another letter he wrote, "I wish I were with you. When you are gone I feel how much you are to me. May God keep you for me for many years to come, if many years are in store for me."[24]

The publication of the story in the press was only the beginning of the public scandal. A committee at Plymouth Church made an investigation in 1874, at which time Theodore Tilton gave a sworn statement accusing his pastor of adultery with his wife. According to some, it was a "hand-picked" committee that "whitewashed" the whole affair; its conclusion was that their pastor was innocent—that there was "nothing whatever in the evidence that should impair the perfect confidence of Plymouth Church or the world in the Christian character and integrity of Henry Ward Beecher."[25]

The next year, Beecher was in city court in Brooklyn in a case brought against him by Tilton. Eunice attended court every day (even when her husband stayed home), giving at least public expression to her support of her husband. In the end, the jury was unable to reach a verdict—a conclusion that was hardly an exoneration of the famous preacher. He went back to his pulpit, yet all but his loyal followers thought him guilty. Four years later, Elizabeth Tilton, by then separated from her husband, wrote a letter confessing that she had lied when she denied having committing adultery with Henry.[26]

How could a preacher remain in the pulpit after such publicity? Beecher had a charismatic personality, and his loyal followers were determined to protect him no matter what the consequences. He likewise had a dutiful wife, who, despite her personality flaws, remained devoted to her husband—and perhaps more importantly, devoted to the ideal of the perfect family. Her own situation obviously did not bear any resemblance to such, but she was determined to present that façade publicly and to promote the ideal.

Eunice no doubt had more than a few suspicions regarding her husband's conduct with other women, but for her own well-being she had no other real choice than to support him. In her day, divorce for women was something the "feminists" talked about, but no true Christian woman would even entertain the thought. Her duty as a wife—and especially as a pastor's wife, as she perceived it—was to support her husband outwardly no matter how sharp the pain and piercing the doubts deep down inside.

The pain that Eunice felt was mainly inside, and it did not quickly go away after the widely publicized scandal surrounding her husband began to fade from public attention. To a friend she confided, "I live in the past over and over and every little while when talking most cheerfully, such a flood of fiery indignation sweeps over me that I am constantly on the watch lest I lose my self-control and show it."[27]

Eunice's difficulty in coping was exacerbated by her husband's treatment of her. In 1876, after the trial, Beecher permitted his son and daughter-in-law to move into their home and turned over the direction of the household to his daughter-in-law. Beecher himself was away on lecture tours much of the time, and he insisted that Eunice spend the winter months in Florida for her health. She resented this deeply, as a letter to him indicates:

> It is very bitter to go away from you, worse now than years ago, because while under this mysterious cloud, whatever it may be, and feeling its cruelty, I am in danger of that which will be far worse than death, that my love and trust in you may grow cold or waver. . . . If your heart has not changed woefully, you would not—you could not subject me to the torture of the last four years.[28]

Many women in similar circumstances might have become bitter and even rebelled against God, but Eunice had an amazing ability to rise above the situation and to go on with life despite the scandal that had so engulfed her family life. Indeed, she had an ability to extract that which was good in her marriage and family life and offer it to others. She did this in her writing, which focused on the home and family. An example is a short article she wrote for the *Ladies' Home Journal* in 1892. As usual, she highlighted her late husband, but the message was powerful and one that was desperately needed in American homes during that period.

The theme of the article was the disciplining of children, and she told how as young parents they had determined to be very strict with their children—not sparing the rod when they misbehaved. But as the years passed, and especially as they endured the grief of losing four of their children, their hearts began to soften. "Little Georgie's loss was a very severe trial, and through the sorrow we were led to a milder interpretation of parental duties." Katie's death was equally painful: "Each year Mr. Beecher was more and more convinced that faults and wrong doing were more truly overcome by loving kindness than by punishment." Then the twins died, and according to Eunice, "from that date I do not think Mr. Beecher ever resorted to corporal punishment."[29]

It is impossible to assess the influence of this article on American families, but it may have touched countless hearts and prevented many physical and psychological scars of child abuse—a problem that had hardly been identified as a crime in that era.

During the last years of their marriage, Beecher permitted Eunice once again to run their household, but he often complained bitterly that she held too tight a reign on his spending. He was known for his extravagance, and she was more of an economizer. It was another aspect of the philosophical differences that they had endured throughout their marriage. Eunice outlived her husband by several years, and she made the best of her circumstances. Her husband had basked in adulation and wallowed in humiliation. As his wife, she shared both and endured amazingly well.

MARGARET SIMPSON

Margaret Simpson
Living With
an Impractical Visionary

It is often the impractical visionaries and creative geniuses in this world who are acclaimed for their success and contributions to society. They receive celebration and fame, while those closest to them are sometimes the most miserable and unhappy of people. This is true in the church as well as in society at large. Mary Livingstone was living in London, friendless and penniless and rumored to be drowning her sorrows in alcohol, while her explorer-husband David was receiving accolades everywhere he went. The tragic ironies were just as great for Bob Pierce, founder of World Vision, and his wife, Lorraine. These men made great names for themselves while their wives—whose names we would never know but for their husbands—suffered in obscurity.

"Sad, but true," writes Denise Turner. "There are ministers who never slow down long enough to be fathers, ministers who are too busy changing the world ever to think about changing a diaper. Then one day, the future slips up and catches them off guard. It is an old story, but it is a story that continues to repeat itself over and over again."[1]

Margaret Simpson was married to such a man, and she and her children suffered as a result.

"The wife of a prophet has no easy road to travel. She cannot always see her husband's vision, yet as his wife she must go along with him wherever his vision takes him. She is compelled therefore to walk by faith a good part of the time—and her husband's faith at that." These were the lines A. W. Tozer used to describe the predicament in which Margaret Simpson found herself. "Mr. Simpson had heard the Voice ordering him out," wrote Tozer, "and he went without fear. His wife had heard nothing, but she was compelled to go anyway. That she was a bit unsympathetic at times has been held against her by many. That she managed to keep within far sight of her absentminded high soaring husband should be set down to her everlasting honor."[2]

Margaret met Albert Benjamin Simpson when he arrived in Toronto to attend seminary. Her father was an elder at Cooke's Presbyterian Church, and he agreed to help out Albert and his brother by offering them inexpensive accommodations in his home. Both brothers were immediately attracted to Margaret, but Albert, with his "handsome features, gracious manners and richly resonant voice . . . won the contest." They waited until his three-year seminary course was over to marry, but meanwhile Albert had many opportunities to demonstrate his romantic inclinations. Although he had trouble meeting his seminary expenses, he managed to buy her presents—once spending the entire ten-dollar honorarium he received from preaching on an expensive gift for her. She was attracted to his sensitive and romantic nature, but those very characteristics created stress in their marriage.[3]

Simpson had a very high-strung and emotional temperament, and he was not physically well much of the time. Some years before he met Margaret, he had a near physical and mental collapse: "Then came a fearful crash in which it seemed to me the very heavens were falling," he later wrote. "After retiring one night suddenly a star appeared to blaze before my eyes; and as I gazed, my nerves gave way. I sprang from my bed trembling and almost fainting with a sense of impending death, then fell into a congestive chill of great violence that lasted all night and almost took my life."[4]

There would be many more times of deep emotional stress for Simpson throughout his life, and Margaret learned early that she would have to adjust to his highs and lows.

Like many new pastors' wives, she was utterly unprepared.

Her husband had trained in seminary and had learned to preach in tiny churches and midweek meetings, but for her role there was no such training ground. When she said "I do" to the preacher, she was automatically thrust into her new role. Indeed, their wedding was the same week that Simpson began his first pastorate at the three-hundred-member Knox Presbyterian Church in Hamilton, Ontario. "Margaret, with no preparation for the pastorate but her conversion, Christian home and high school education, stood at the entrance of an uncertain future."[5]

During Simpson's early years of ministry, Margaret enjoyed the recognition her husband was receiving. He was sensational as a young Presbyterian preacher and was quickly earmarked for greatness by many of his listeners. During his eight years in Hamilton, some 750 new members joined the church, and new programs were initiated.[6]

With his widely acclaimed success, Simpson began receiving calls from other churches, and after a painful farewell in 1873, he and his family moved to Louisville, Kentucky. There he served as pastor of the Chestnut Street Church, the largest Presbyterian church in the city. In many ways it was a difficult move for Margaret, but the promise of a five-thousand-dollar annual salary brightened her prospects. With three little children and another soon to come, that generous salary was welcomed.[7]

Although Simpson had believed himself called to pastoral ministry, he was very sensitive to other possibilities that God might have in store for him. Foreign missions weighed heavily on his mind, and it was during his Louisville ministry that he experienced a visionary, personal "call" to overseas evangelism. It happened while he was away attending a conference.

> I was awakened one night from sleep, trembling with a strange and solemn sense of God's overshadowing power, and on my soul was burning the remembrance of a strange dream through which I had that moment come. It seemed to me that I was sitting in a vast auditorium, and millions of people were there sitting around me. All the Christians in the world seemed to be there, and on the platform was a great multitude of faces and forms. They seemed to be mostly Chinese. They were not speaking but in mute anguish were wringing their hands, and their faces wore an expression that I can never forget. . . . As I awoke with that vision on my mind, I did tremble

with the Holy Spirit, and I threw myself on my knees and every fibre of my being answered, "Yes, Lord, I will go."[8]

Simpson immediately sent word to Margaret of his decision to become a foreign missionary. Her reaction was swift: "I was not then ready for such a sacrifice. I wrote to him that it was all right— he might go to China himself—I would remain at home and support and care for the children. I knew that would settle him for a while."[9]

That did settle him, but only "for a while"—as Margaret was soon to find out. It is worth noting, however, that Simpson did not on this occasion ignore his wife's concerns. That has not been true of some great missionary pioneers, including C. T. Studd, who left his invalid wife in England to begin a mission in Africa.

From the beginning of his ministry in Louisville, Simpson was an innovator with new ideas to reach out more effectively to the unbelievers in that city. He began holding evangelistic campaigns and after only one year proposed that a large tabernacle be built to accommodate the new outreach. The original plans were soon enlarged, so that by the time of its completion in 1878, the tabernacle was large enough to seat more than two thousand. But despite his growing popularity and the evidence of his success, after less than six years in Louisville, Simpson resigned to accept a call to New York City.[10]

Simpson's decision to leave was difficult not only for the church but for Margaret as well. She had grown to love the church and the financial security it offered, and she was fearful about the prospects of moving to New York with no definite ministry in mind and was upset with her husband's inclination toward independent city ministries. Likewise, she feared for her children and the evil influences they would encounter in the nation's largest city. She was vehemently opposed to the move, as entries in Simpson's diary during this period show. And Simpson's editorial reference to "a long and almost overwhelming domestic trial" some months after the move would indicate the problem did not quickly pass.[11]

Simpson was convinced he was following direct orders from God, and thus his wife's opinion counted for little. Indeed, he "gave no more heed to her opposition than he did to that of the congregation. In his diary entry of November 10, 1879, he wrote: 'Tonight my pastorate was dissolved by the presbytery and I am Christ's free servant.'" He and Margaret and the four children left for New York by train, not knowing where their next paycheck was coming from. Simpson was a popular preacher, however, and his reputation had preceded him; within a week he had a unanimous call from the Thirteenth Street Presbyterian Church.[12]

Margaret's frustration with moving to New York City was compounded by her husband's poor health. The second year of the ministry there was clouded by Simpson's prolonged absence from the pulpit. "Along with the physical and nervous prostration came mental gloom. He took a leave of absence from the church and went to Saratoga Springs, but nothing seemed to help. 'I was deeply depressed,' he confessed, 'and all things in life looked dark and withered.'"[13] Needless to say, it was a difficult time for Margaret, left alone with four young children in a city where she did not feel at home.

Soon after this period of deep depression and physical exhaustion, Simpson attended a healing service in Old Orchard, Maine. There he heard messages and testimonies that were new to him, and after a period of contemplation he claimed the doctrine of divine healing for himself. His testimony as to his own healing came as a welcome relief to his wife and friends, but the real test of his newfound commitment occurred soon after he and his family returned from Maine.

The Simpsons' younger daughter, three-year-old Margaret, became severely ill with diphtheria. Mrs. Simpson was frantic. Years before, the couple had lost their second son to the same disease when he was the same age as little Margaret. But Simpson insisted they trust God alone for her healing: "That night, with a throat white as snow and a raging fever, the little sufferer lay beside me alone. I knew that if the sickness lasted to the following day there would be a crisis in my family. With trembling hand I anointed her brow and claimed the power of Jesus' name." The next morning there was a significant improvement in her health, and Simpson was convinced he had won his point on the issue of healing.[14]

Simpson's biographer, A. E. Thompson, has claimed that for Mrs. Simpson this "was a turning point in her life" and that she rallied behind her husband in his ministry, but other evidence would indicate that some of her deepest struggles were yet ahead of her. Soon after this incident (and just two years after he had announced to his Louisville congregation that he would be moving to New York), he announced at Thirteenth Street Presbyterian Church that he had applied Luke 4:18 to himself: "The Spirit of the Lord is upon me because he has anointed me to preach the gospel to the poor." That "call," in addition to his reservations about certain points of Presbyterian doctrine, sealed his fate and concluded his ministry at the church.[15]

As much as Margaret had dreaded the move to New York, the pastorate at the Thirteenth Street church had at least afforded a semblance of stability and financial security. This latest decision, however, was a nightmare to her. The morning after her husband had given his startling sermon, the elders visited her at home "to express their profound sympathy." Simpson later reflected that "they remarked as they condoled with her that they felt they were attending his funeral," and he himself conjectured that "it is possible she may have felt that he might as well be dead."[16]

Margaret's fears were well-founded. She was suddenly plunged into desperate financial straits. *His* ministry was to preach to the poor—a ministry that required no outlay of funds. *Her* ministry was to care for the needs of a husband, five children, and herself—a ministry that entailed significant expense. In one day his income had gone from five thousand dollars a year to nothing. Needless to say, Margaret was distressed. In her mind, her husband's unilateral decision was rash and foolhardy.

> From one of the most prestigious and influential pulpits of the nation's leading city, he stepped into seeming oblivion. He found himself alone in a great city known even then for its expensive ways; he had no following, no backing, no prospects of employment and no visible means of carrying out the vision that had propelled him to such a drastic step.[17]

As rash as his decision was, hindsight reveals that it was this decision that launched Simpson into the great venture for which he has since become known. Had he remained a Presbyterian minister, his name would probably have been lost in history and the great missionary movement that he founded—the Christian and Missionary Alliance—would never have come into being. Yet the initial weeks and months of his independent ministry were very shaky. On the first Sunday in the new venture, he preached to a group of people who gathered to hear what his plans for outreach were. At this time he invited everyone who was interested in helping him to meet the following Wednesday. "Five women and two men responded," none of whom "had an annual income exceeding $300"; one was a recently converted drunkard. They met in a chilly, third-floor dance hall, convinced God would honor their faith.[18]

Within three months Simpson had organized an independent church, "The Gospel Tabernacle," with thirty-five charter members. The little group grew rapidly, despite confusion and instability in the early years. During the first eight years, the group met at twelve locations in all. In 1889, a large permanent structure was completed, and from that time the church became a center of home and foreign mission work in New York City. Simpson finally had his own independent pulpit, where he could preach and develop programs without denominational restrictions. It was also a place where his fame as a preacher grew. After visiting New York, D. L. Moody told a friend, "I have just been down to hear A. B. Simpson preach. No one gets to my heart like that man."[19]

The early years of independence were very difficult for Margaret, as she later recalled:

> We had moved from the comfortable Manse on Thirty-second Street to a little four-room apartment. One morning we had nothing for breakfast but oatmeal. Not being able to trust the Lord as my husband was doing, I went out and for the first time in my life ordered supplies for which I could not pay. For some days Mr. Simpson received very little money. Sometimes he would come in with a small piece of meat or some other necessity. One morning I received a letter from a lady in Philadelphia, whom I did not know, containing a check for one hundred and fifty dollars. I hurried over to the church office to have Mr. Simpson cash it at a neighboring bank, and then made the rounds of the stores to pay the bills.[20]

Although the Simpsons' financial circumstances improved as time went on, there continued to be some serious philosophical differences between Margaret and her visionary husband. As

Simpson became more and more involved in a healing ministry, he encouraged others to follow his lead and to open healing centers in their homes. He himself wanted to turn his home into a physical and spiritual healing retreat center, but Margaret vehemently opposed the idea and won her point. "Their children should be raised in a home, she argued, not an institution."[21]

The risks involved in rearing children in New York City had been one of Margaret's strongest objections to moving there. In the late nineteenth century there was a widespread phobia of city life among Protestants, and Margaret reflected that mindset. It is to her husband's credit that, unlike most Protestants of the era, he had a vision for reaching the teeming millions in the cities.

That her children would be ruined by city life was probably an unwarranted fear of Margaret's. The greater fear, which was far more justified and over which she seemed to have less control, was that her children would be ruined due to lack of fatherly influence. A. W. Tozer reflected on this problem: "The difficulties Simpson later experienced in bringing his children to Christ may be attributed in part to the fact that they had been sacrificed too far in the interest of their father's public ministry."[22]

When they moved to New York the Simpsons had four children. "Albert Henry by now was thirteen; James Gordon, nine; Mabel Jane, seven; and Margaret May, not quite two." Whether it was the city or the home environment, Margaret's "fears would prove justified. Both Albert and James later succumbed to the temptation rampant in New York City. A third son, Howard Home, would be born in New York and prove just as susceptible to its temptations as his older brothers. They would not return to the Lord until their last days."[23] The "last days" for the two older brothers did not occur in old age. Albert Henry died before he reached the age of thirty, and James Gordon, at the age of thirty-seven.[24]

As a mother and pastor's wife, Margaret had served faithfully. As the "wife of a prophet," as A. W. Tozer called her, she served as a critic and opponent at times. Like his loyal followers (who numbered in the thousands before his death), she recognized her husband's genius, but unlike them she had to live with him and endure his eccentricities at a personal, day-to-day level. "He would soar, and she would struggle. His vision of the heavenlies at times would obscure his earthly duties as father and husband, while her practical preoccupations would at times allow no honor for the prophet in his own home."[25]

Margaret mellowed in her attitude toward her husband's ministry as the work stabilized and the children grew to adulthood, but she was not as committed to the ministry as several other women were. Carrie Judd faithfully supported Simpson in his healing ministry, opening healing centers of her own; Sophie Lichtenfels was a dynamic speaker and city mission worker; May Stephens was his songleader and pianist, wrote hymns, and pioneered the work with the Eighth Avenue Mission; and Emma Whittemore founded The Door of Hope Missions throughout the world. "Ladies teamed up for house-to-house visitation and special meetings for 'fallen women.' The South Street Mission was one of at least four havens begun through their efforts."[26]

Because of these other women, Margaret Simpson had very little impact on the ministry for which her husband became known, and she has been the target of severe criticism by many who felt she was not the supportive wife she should have been. In her later years she did, according to Gerald McGraw, "become reconciled to her husband's calling, loyally backing him even if she often did not share his dreams. Eventually she shared the platform with him and became very active in promoting the Christian causes he had originated."[27]

Still, Margaret suffered when her husband suffered and bore the brunt of his near manic-depressive personality. "It is characteristic of the God-intoxicated, the dreamers and mystics of the Kingdom," wrote A. W. Tozer, "that their flight-range is greater than that of other men. Their ability to sweep upward to unbelievable heights of spiritual transport is equaled only by their sad power to descend, to sit in dazed dejection by the River Chebar or to startle the night watches with their lonely grief." Even in the final months of his life, Simpson suffered from deep depression and "went under a spiritual cloud. He felt that the face of the Lord was hidden from him, and he mourned as one who had suffered the loss of his last and dearest treasure."[28] Margaret was there to the end, always standing by and hoping for the best, but never able to comprehend fully the man she had married fifty-four years earlier.

• PART III •
MINISTRY CHALLENGES

W hat many women view as a problem, others see as a challenge. Indeed, there is sometimes a fine line between problems and challenges. Susanna Wesley faced what otherwise might have been a devastating problem—marital breakdown—with *chutzpah* (a Yiddish term for fortitude, nerve, and gall). She perfected her own gifts of preaching and teaching and the training of her children as a result of her husband's neglect. The problem remained, and she and her family suffered because of it; but she did not allow it to consume her and destroy her own initiative.

In his book *The Road Less Traveled,* M. Scott Peck, a psychiatrist, maintains that problems are the very basis on which individuals develop and mature. "Problems are the cutting edge that distinguishes between success and failure. Problems call forth our courage and our wisdom; indeed, they create our courage and our wisdom. It is only because of problems that we grow mentally and spiritually. . . . It is through the pain of confronting and resolving problems that we learn."[1]

Betty Coble, writing to pastors' wives, emphasizes the heavy price they must pay if they become consumed in their problems. "There are many things that cannot be changed," she writes. "It is easier but more costly just to be upset with what you cannot change than to take charge of yourself and work with those things that are changeable."[2]

There are some things, however, that might appear unchangeable, but with the right amount of *chutzpah* can be turned around. Susannah Spurgeon was distressed over negative press reports about her husband. Although she was an invalid, she took up the challenge to let the world know what kind of a man she was married to and began distributing his books and sermons. The reputation Spurgeon has today as one of the great preachers of the nineteenth century is due in part to the efforts made by his loyal wife.

Emma Moody also rose to the challenge of changing what others might have regarded as unchangeable. She was determined that her husband's social graces, his grammar, his dress, and his general demeanor be upgraded so that he could move in circles that would enhance his ministry and in turn enhance the work of God.

Daisy Smith faced a decision that is harder for most women today than it was for her in the early decades of the twentieth century. She gave up her own effective public ministry to devote her time to her husband and family. In doing so, Daisy encountered many struggles, but she faced the challenge and became a much-admired "first lady" in one of the most missionary-oriented churches in modern times.

Catherine Marshall, unlike Daisy Smith, married a man who had already acquired fame. Though she was eminently gifted herself, she stayed in the background and was not recognized until after her husband's death; only then did she take up the challenge to develop and exercise her own gifts in writing and speaking, which led her to far greater international prominence than her husband had ever attained.

For Ruth Peale, who was married to the preacher most known for positive thinking, the challenge was to keep her husband from discouragement. Like so many great men, he suffered from periods of gloom and despair, and it was her positive spirit that brought him through many of these times.

Jill Briscoe's challenge was to find a place for herself in ministry while married to a man who was consumed in ministry of his own. The struggle was made easier by his strong support of her and her gifts, but it was not easy during her early years of marriage, when he was gone for months at a time. She rose to the challenge, however, and has developed a model for partnership in ministry that has been effectively sustained at Elmbrook Church. She serves as an inspiration to pastors' wives everywhere to turn difficulties into success—to take up the challenge of ministry and find happiness in serving others.

SUSANNAH SPURGEON

Susannah Spurgeon
Presenting a Proper Image to the Press

That the first lady of the parish would become involved in presenting a proper image of her husband to the press should not come as a surprise to anyone. First ladies seem to gravitate naturally toward that responsibility. It has certainly been true of first ladies in the White House. In an article entitled "The Week of the Dragon," *Time* magazine reported that Nancy Reagan was attracting attention for her efforts to protect the President. Howard Baker, the new chief of staff, reportedly said that when she "gets her hackles up, she can be a dragon."[1] An Associated Press article on the same subject, entitled "First Ladies Always Have Been Protective," speaks of Woodrow Wilson's wife and other first ladies in the same vein. "The scenario is familiar: the presidency is in crisis, and the first lady" becomes defensive— "battling to protect her man."[2]

The pastor's wife often ends up in a situation similar to that of the President's wife. Because she is so closely associated with her husband's ministry, she finds herself taking on a defensive posture where he is concerned. One pastor's wife summed it up by saying, "We are involved with promoting parish approval and dispelling parish criticism."[3]

As different as their husbands were, there were some

significant similarities between Eunice Beecher and Susannah Spurgeon—especially in the way they responded to the publicity surrounding their husbands. Both sought to build up the image of the famous preachers to whom they were married, and both became involved in writing their late husbands' life stories.

Susannah Spurgeon was the wife of one of the most famous Baptist preachers of all time. Charles Haddon Spurgeon began preaching as a youth, and by the time he was nineteen he had gained such a wide reputation for preaching that he was asked to fill the recently vacated pulpit of the New Park Street Church in London. Soon afterward he officially became the pastor. Within a short time the church had grown so large that new accommodations were needed, and the Metropolitan Tabernacle was built to meet the need.

When Spurgeon first came to New Park Street, he was single, but that did not last for long. Within months after he began his ministry, he declared his love and proposed marriage to Susie Thompson, one of his parishioners, and a year and a half later, in 1856, they were married.[4]

Susie's initial reaction to Spurgeon was amusement more than admiration. A cultured young woman two years his senior, she was the daughter of a well-to-do ribbon manufacturer and was impressed neither by his looks nor his dress. His speaking style, likewise, did not meet her taste, but she soon realized he was a young man with great potential, and it did not take long for him to win her heart.[5]

Susie learned early in her marriage that she would not always receive all the attention she wanted from her preoccupied preacher-husband. The story is told that at times he was so preoccupied that he greeted and shook hands with her as she entered the church, as though she were a total stranger.[6] Susie, needless to say, had a difficult time adjusting. On one occasion she and Spurgeon became separated in a crowd of well-wishers as he was entering an auditorium to speak, and he forgot all about her. She later reflected on the incident:

> "At first, I was utterly bewildered, and then . . . I was *angry*. I at once returned home, and told my grief to my gentle mother. . . . She wisely reasoned that my chosen husband was no ordinary man,

that his whole life was absolutely dedicated to God and His service, and that I must never, *never* hinder him by trying to put myself first in his heart."[7]

This seeming callousness toward Susie did not reflect a spirit of indifference on Spurgeon's part. Indeed, he could be a gushing romantic, as the opening lines of a poem he wrote for her several years after they were married illustrate:

> Over the space that parts us, my wife,
>   I'll cast me a bridge of song;
> Our hearts shall meet, O joy of my life,
>   On its arch, unseen, but strong.
>
> The wooer his new love's name may wear
>   Engraved on a precious stone,
> But thine image within my heart I bear,
>   The heart that has long been thine own.[8]

The deep affection that the Spurgeons had for each other helped them to minister to each other under difficult circumstances. The greatest sorrow of their ministry occurred during their first year of marriage. Spurgeon's popularity had soared to the point that temporary quarters were needed before the Metropolitan Tabernacle was completed. A large music hall was rented, and crowds packed the seats and aisles. Just as Spurgeon was beginning one sermon, someone in the crowd shouted, "Fire!" Panic and pandemonium ensued. Before the bedlam was over, seven had died and many others were critically injured. Susie, having stayed at home with month-old twins, learned of this "black shadow of sorrow which the Lord saw fit to cast over our young and happy lives" when a deacon arrived at the door:

> I wanted to be alone, that I might cry to God in this hour of darkness and death! When my beloved was brought home, he looked a wreck of his former self—an hour's agony of mind had changed his whole appearance and bearing. The night that ensued was one of weeping, and wailing, and indescribable sorrow. He refused to be comforted. I thought the morning would never break; and when it did come, it brought no relief.[9]

The story made the headlines of the newspapers, some of which reported the incident sympathetically, others heartlessly.

One wrote of the "vile blasphemies" that were heard "above the cries of the dead and the dying, and louder than the wails of misery from the maimed and suffering" that "resounded from the mouth of Spurgeon." The article added that

> when the mangled corpses had been carried away from the unhallowed and disgraceful scene . . . the clink of money as it fell into the collection-boxes grated harshly, miserably, on the ears of those who, we sincerely hope, have by this time conceived for Mr. Spurgeon and his rantings the profoundest contempt.[10]

The sorrow of that night was a heartache the Spurgeons never got over.

Susie had many health problems, which often prevented her from traveling with her husband. According to one historian, "she was a victim of what has been described as 'that morbid realm of Victorian illness which is likely to escape modern understanding entirely.'"[11] Apparently she suffered from some gynecological malady, of which she was never fully cured.

Although she had children (her twin sons, Charles and Thomas) and the church provided luxurious living quarters, Susie found the times when her husband was away very difficult. "These separations," she wrote later on, "were very painful to hearts so tenderly united as were ours, but we each bore our share of the sorrow as heroically as we could, and softened it as far as possible by constant correspondence." Spurgeon rarely missed a day in writing to her and often included his own sketched drawings depicting people and places he had visited. As his popularity grew, the frequency of his travels and his separations from Susie both increased.[12]

As popular as Spurgeon was, he was often the butt of ridicule and scorn in the press. Nineteenth-century newspapers were far more blunt and sarcastic in both their editorial and news columns than they are today, so it was not uncommon for Susie to read articles such as the one printed in the *Essex Standard* about her husband's early ministry:

> His style is that of the vulgar colloquial, varied by rant. . . . All the most solemn mysteries of our holy religion are by him rudely, roughly and impiously handled. Mystery is vulgarized, sanctity profaned, common sense outraged and decency disgusted. . . . His

rantings are interspersed with course anecdotes that split the ears of groundlings; and this is popularity! This is the "religious furor" of London![13]

Spurgeon was not entirely without blame. He was outrageous in some of his mannerisms, and dogmatic and critical in his theology. He was a strong Calvinist who had nothing but condemnation for those who disagreed: "Arminian perversions, in particular, are to sink back to their birthplace in the pit." He minced no words in his scorn of the belief that one could lose his salvation: it was "the wickedest falsehood on earth."[14]

For Susie, the primary role of the pastor's wife was to support her husband in his ministry. The particular aspect of ministry for which her husband was best known was, of course, preaching, and in this regard she played a vital role. In preparing his sermons, Spurgeon wrote, "my habit is to look to the Lord for guidance, and when a text comes with power to my soul, I take it without hesitation." Once the text was determined, he called Susie into the library, as she recalled:

> For some time it has been the dear Pastor's custom, as soon as the text has been given him of the Master, to call me into the study and permit me to read the various commentaries on the subject-matter. My heart has burned within me. . . . I listened to his dear voice condensing the old Puritans in whom he delights. Thus a poor prisoner [referring to her invalid state] has the first sip of the wine— the first morsel from the loaves with which the thousands are to be fed on the morrow.

Of these times, Spurgeon himself wrote: "She reads . . . and gradually I am guided as to the best form of outline!"[15]

On one occasion, while he was struggling particularly hard to develop the meaning of a biblical text, Spurgeon took a rest at Susie's prompting. "Worn out by his efforts, he fell into a deep sleep, and then began to deliver a sermon." It was "a clear and distinct exposition of its [the text's] meaning, with much force and freshness." Realizing what was happening, Susie immediately began taking notes, "and was able to present her waking spouse with a fully prepared sermon outline. . . . The story strains credibility," writes Patricia Kruppa, "but both were fond of repeating it as a factual instance of a wonder-working providence."[16]

Although she was often in a semi-invalid state of health and was unable even to attend church services at the Tabernacle, Susannah Spurgeon had an important ministry of her own, one in a sense that directly counteracted the negative press to which her husband was subject. In 1875, after his volume *Lectures to My Students* was published, she vowed it would be her ministry to "send a copy to every minister in England." She initially paid the costs from her household budget, but as the project grew, others began contributing. Then other writings, including the four-volume *Treasury of David,* were sent to pastors. Within a few months she had sent more than three thousand books to "pastors of all denominations," and after three years the number was approaching twenty thousand. One of her most passionate objectives was to get the books into the hands of poor curates in the Church of England.[17]

Shortly after she initiated the ministry, Susie gave a melodramatic account of the importance of the work:

> . . . But, ah! dear friends, when I look at the list of names, I see the only shadow of sadness that ever rests upon my Book-Fund. It is the grief of knowing that there exists a terrible necessity for this service of love; that without this help . . . the poor pastors to whom it has been sent must have gone on famishing for mental food, their incomes being so wretchedly small that they scarcely know how to "provide things honest" for themselves and their families, while the money for the purchase of books is absolutely unobtainable.
>
> It is most touching to hear some tell with eloquence the effect the gift produced upon them. One is "not ashamed to say" he received the parcel with "tears of joy," wife and children standing around and rejoicing with him. Another, as soon as the wrappings fall from the precious volumes, praises God aloud and sings the Doxology with all his might; while a third, when his eyes light on the long-coveted "Treasury of David," "rushes from the room" that he may go alone and "pour out his full heart before his God."[18]

Unlike the ministry of some pastors' wives, Susie's was certainly no threat to her husband. He was clearly the luminary in the household, and hers was a supporting ministry—specifically geared to bolster his ministry and to meet the journalistic assaults with a forceful counterattack. Spurgeon expressed his appreciation to her publicly in his widely circulated magazine *The Sword and Trowel,* crediting her with time-consuming and important ministry:

> It is one of the delights of my life that my beloved wife has made ministers' libraries her great concern. The dear soul gives herself wholly to it. You should see her stores, her book-room, her busy helpers on the parcel-day, and the wagon-load of books each fortnight. The Book Fund at certain hours is the ruling idea of our house. Every day it occupies the head and heart of its manager. The reader has scant idea of the book-keeping involved in the book-giving; but this may be said,—the loving manager has more than 6000 names on her lists, and yet she knows every volume that each man has received from the first day till now. The work is not muddled, but done as if by clockwork, yet it is performed with a hearty desire to give pleasure to all receivers and to trouble no applicant with needless inquiries.[19]

Another ministry that Susannah initiated was the Sermon Fund. Though far less extensive than the Book Fund, it had a similar purpose: to circulate Spurgeon's teachings. Some of the sermons were translated into other languages, and funds were designated for overseas distribution. A missionary from Syria wrote to Susie that "about 1,500 copies of Sermons had been distributed to school children in the homes of the town, after they had been exhorted by their teachers to read them to their parents."[20]

In addition to the Book Fund, Susie was responsible for the Pastors' Aid Fund, which was established "to help the families of needy ministers in England by sending them suitable parcels of clothing." Like many Christian women before her, she strictly avoided sectarianism. "Not least among the many recommendations of this noble enterprise," wrote George Needham, "is the catholicity of its scope. In days when sectarian rancor often runs high, and there is much division in the Christian camp, we cannot be too thankful for any agency that obliterates these dividing lines by the overflowing tide of sympathy and help."[21]

If nonsectarianism characterized Susie's ministry, the same could not be said for her husband's. He was as quick to lash out against his fellow Baptists as against the Anglicans and the Arminians. The most contentious theological controversy of his career erupted in 1887 and became known as the "Down-Grade" controversy. Perhaps he had hardened over the years, but in this conflict "he seems to have had much less kindliness in his attitudes" than he had manifested in earlier times. "His opponents were 'the adversaries of the Lord,'" and he began to make specific charges of heresy against certain preachers and called on fellow Baptists to withdraw from the British Baptist Union.[22]

Spurgeon had expected an outpouring of support, but instead "the Union passed a vote of censure upon him," and he lost many longtime friends. "In the judgement of many it was a needless sorrow to both sides," wrote a biographer. "Susannah felt that the controversy cost him his life," and Spurgeon himself remarked to a friend, "you will never see me again; this fight is killing me."[23]

The criticism that Susie had to deal with related not only to her husband's preaching style and theology, but also to his lifestyle. This included the censure of his drinking alcoholic beverages and his smoking habit. In 1863 an American temperance activist harshly criticized his social drinking, but the most publicized attacks came more than a decade later. In 1874 a Baptist minister from America was visiting the Metropolitan Tabernacle. He was invited to join Spurgeon on the platform and to give a challenge to the congregation at the end of the sermon— to personally apply Spurgeon's remarks to his own life and the lives of the listeners.

Spurgeon's sermon addressed "strongly and plainly upon the necessity of giving up sin"—sins that included unconscious habits that were displeasing to God. Apparently not knowing that Spurgeon himself smoked, the visiting minister responded to the sermon by relating how he had once smoked, but had since renounced the habit in order to live a life more pleasing to the Lord. "Throughout his words ran the idea that smoking was not only an enslaving habit, but that the Christian must look on it as a sin."[24]

How should the most famous preacher in the land respond to such a rebuke? It was no secret that Spurgeon smoked a cigar while driving to his study at the Tabernacle each morning. There is no doubt that the best response would have been no response (*or* a confession that his habit was indeed wrong, and a renunciation of it), and that is no doubt the response Susie would have wished for.

But Spurgeon was both impulsive and defensive, and he was unable to let the remarks go unchallenged. "Well, dear friends, you know that some men can do to the glory of God what to other men would be a sin. And, notwithstanding what Brother Pentecost has said, I intend to smoke a good cigar to the glory of God before I go to bed to-night."[25]

Spurgeon should not have been surprised that the press would publicize the story all over England. In response to the publicity, he further defended his practice, digging himself deeper into the predicament. Although he apparently gave up smoking before he died, it was not until after his picture had been used in cigar advertising.

Luxurious living was another sore point in later years. In 1880 the Spurgeons moved to a nine-acre suburban estate. The house was "a typical Victorian gentleman's home," and the grounds were wooded with "an abundance of flowers and shrubs, together with a garden, stables, . . . pasture," and "a small scenic pond." It quickly became an issue for reproach. "Exaggerated descriptions of the house and the grounds were circulated, and it was said Spurgeon lived in a home fit for a prince. . . . An American minister, after visiting London, likened the estate to that of Buckingham Palace."[26]

In the eyes of some people, Spurgeon was extravagant with his wife. He bought Susie jewels and other nice gifts that were far beyond the means of the majority of people in his congregation. It was just one way, however, that he chose to demonstrate his love for her. "To the end of their lives, they were lovers," writes a biographer, "and what could be more touching than these two old invalids, she grown plump and looking slightly absurd wearing the girlish curls, he prematurely tired and aged, yet writing each other love poems as though they were still twenty and courting."[27]

Despite her poor health, Susie outlived her husband by a decade. During these years, she spent much of her time in editing his autobiography, a work that was truly a labor of love.[28] That project, like her entire married life, was dedicated to bolstering her husband in the eyes of the public. She believed more than anyone that he was truly God's servant, and thus she poured herself into enhancing his ministry by enhancing his image.

She was ever-conscious of the press. Even before their

marriage she began making a collection of all the articles that were written about him, and many of those were included in the autobiography she edited. In that volume she wrote of her personal struggle with her husband's critics.

No defence of my beloved is needed now. God has taken him to Himself, and "there the wicked cease from troubling; and there the weary be at rest." The points of these arrows are all blunted — the stings of these scorpions are all plucked out. . . .

A strange serenity has brooded over my spirit as these chapters have recalled the heartless attacks made on God's servant; I have even smiled as I read once again the unjust and cruel words written by his enemies; for he is so safe now. . . .

But, at the time of their publication, what a grievous affliction these slanders were to me! My heart alternately sorrowed over him, and flamed with indignation against his detractors. For a long time, I wondered how I could set continual comfort before his eyes, till, at last, I hit upon the expedient of having the following verses printed in large Old English type, and enclosed in a pretty Oxford frame:

"Blessed are ye, when men shall revile you, and persecute you, and shall say all manner of evil against you falsely, for My sake. Rejoice, and be exceeding glad: for great is your reward in Heaven: for so persecuted they the prophets which were before you." — Matthew V. 11, 12.[29]

EMMA MOODY

• 10 •
Emma Moody
Remaking a Man for Ministry

How hard should a pastor's wife try to cultivate her husband's personality, intellect, and habits to better qualify him for ministry? The answer to this question depends to some extent on how secure the husband is and whether he is interested in self-improvement. "A wife may have greater verbal skills than her husband, and a sense of correct grammar that is sharper than her husband's," writes Frances Nordland. "I should think a man would value his wife's suggestions or her calling his attention to any mistakes in grammar or pronunciation." She advises wives to be sensitive as to *when* they criticize a husband's sermon delivery— preferably waiting a day to do so.[1]

Betty Coble argues that it is possible for a young pastor's wife to take too seriously her responsibility to "remake" her husband, and she warns against it:

> The term helpmeet is used to describe a wife in a mysteriously spiritual way. Helpmeet to some means that a wife is to help her husband become what God intended him to be. In her mind she is to complete him or make him perfect by her standard. If this is her idea, she immediately sets in to straighten him out. She has a great deal of encouragement from those around her by such statements as, "Behind every successful man is a devoted woman."

I overheard this piece of advice being given to a young minister's wife: "You determine the effectiveness of your husband's ministry." What that young woman heard was, "You are responsible for how your husband relates to God, follows God, relates to people, and leads people." That is not true. Such statements shackle a minister's wife with a burden that is not hers to bear. She does not become responsible for how her husband relates to God or anyone else. She is not responsible for his manners or his thinking. As a wife she is to contribute herself to the building of her marriage. In marriage both persons remain responsible for themselves and become responsible to their mate in the marriage.[2]

Emma Moody probably would have agreed with that advice, but on the other hand, she was not the kind of woman who would have shrugged in despair at her husband's quirks and eccentricities, convinced that it is not possible to change a man once he becomes a husband.

Although Dwight L. Moody is not remembered primarily as a pastor, he did found a church and served as its first pastor. He was a contemporary of Charles H. Spurgeon whose influence and popularity rivaled that of Spurgeon, but he ever considered himself far below the great preacher of the Metropolitan Tabernacle. Emma Moody, like Susie Spurgeon, saw great potential in her husband, and she dedicated her life to helping him overcome his very obvious deficiencies for public ministry.

Emma Revell first became acquainted with Moody when, as a shy thirteen-year-old, she was teaching a girls' Sunday school class at the First Baptist Church in Chicago. Moody's own church was Plymouth Congregational, but one church was not enough for him. He was involved in a young men's class at the Methodist Episcopal church and in "drumming up scholars" for the Baptists at the Wells Street Mission. That had been his first venture in Christian service. "They trooped behind as Moody hurried through courts and alleys until, sweaty and triumphant, he delivered to Wells Street no less than eighteen ragged boys, most of them barefoot."[3]

At fifteen, Emma also became involved in evangelistic outreach and teaching at the Wells Street Mission, and it was this involvement that led to her lifelong partnership with Moody. Emma Revell was the daughter of Fleming H. Revell, a French

Huguenot who had come to America after residing in London for a time. Although Revell's financial situation was precarious at best, the family had an air of sophistication that would have been intimidating to many young men of Moody's low social standing. Emma, born in London in 1843, in character was the striking opposite of Moody in many ways.

> Moody brimmed with health, strength and energy, an extrovert. Emma suffered already from asthma and headaches, was shy and retiring. His humor was boisterous, hers deep and quietly playful. "No two people were ever more in contrast," their younger son Paul summed up, long after both were dead. "He was impulsive, outspoken, dominant, informal, and with little education at the time they met. She was intensely conventional and conservative, far better educated, fond of reading, with a discriminate taste, and self-effacing to the last degree."[4]

At seventeen, Emma became a schoolteacher, and in that same year she and Dwight became engaged. It came with an awkward public announcement: "Suddenly in 1860, without much warning we find Dwight Moody rising one night in a church service to announce that he has just 'become engaged to Miss Emma Revell, and therefore cannot be depended upon to see the other girls home from meeting.'" In 1862, at nineteen, she and Moody were married.[5]

When she first became attracted to him, he had been a successful shoe salesman, with the dream of earning one hundred thousand dollars. By 1860 he was earning more than five thousand dollars a year in commissions—this during a time when a mechanic earned only a tenth that much. Giving up the prospects of a prosperous livelihood was, in Moody's words, "three months of the severest struggle of my life," but once the decision was made, he enthusiastically plunged into a full-time ministry of inner-city mission work.[6] Emma was well aware that her marriage to Moody would not bring her financial security, but her commitment to ministry and to Moody overcame her fears.

Even before their marriage, Emma began the overwhelming task of "remaking" Moody for ministry. She was not unaware of his gross deficiencies in education and social graces. "She took on Moody's education," according to J. C. Pollock, but never was successful in getting his writing up to standard. He spelled phonetically, and he avoided punctuation altogether.[7] Likewise, he frequently mispronounced words and used bad grammar in his speaking. But Emma, the schoolmarm, was persistent in her mission.

Remaking her husband to meet the minimum of social acceptability was an even more formidable task for Emma. She was never able to turn him into a polished dignitary, but she witnessed amazing progress, considering the raw material she had to work with. After they were married, "she threw away those patent shirts he was so proud of that did not, he claimed, need washing for weeks on end."[8]

As a competent teacher, Emma did not limit her efforts to her husband. She had performed well teaching for the Chicago public school system, and she willingly offered her expertise to Moody's Bible school. On one occasion, when she was seen teaching a men's class of some forty students, a visitor objected—challenging Moody with the impropriety of having a young woman teach such a large group of middle-aged men. Moody responded by saying that it appeared to him as though she was doing a very creditable job of teaching. It was only after the visitor persisted in his opposition that he discovered the woman was Moody's wife.[9]

Emma was, likewise, very competent in personal, one-on-one counseling, and no one appreciated this gift more than Dwight himself: "When I have an especially hard case, I turn him over to my wife; she can bring a man to a decision for Christ where I cannot touch him."[10]

Emma had strong religious convictions, and she had a stabilizing influence on her husband in theological and biblical matters. She also persuaded him to broaden his outlook on certain issues. Moody, a Congregationalist, founded his independent Chicago church according to Congregationalist principles, but Emma persuaded him to allow for a baptistery in addition to the font, so that immersion could be practiced as well as infant baptism by sprinkling.[11]

Besides her public ministry, Emma made a ministry out of being a wife and mother. According to her son, Paul, "She made a home-away-from-home for him [Dwight], shielding him from interruptions, bores and cranks always in abundance; writing his letters; handling all his money; paying his bills; and doing all in her power to set him free for the work he was doing, in which she took the greatest pride and interest."[12]

Emma's role as Moody's private secretary would be difficult to underestimate. She not only handled correspondence and bookings, but also served as a troubleshooter when the situation called for it. One such time was in 1887, when conflict had arisen in Chicago over the direction the Evangelization Society, over which Moody presided, should move in as new opportunities arose. Moody had been away for an extended period, and Mrs. Cyrus McCormick had sought to serve as a mediator between the opposing factions. She corresponded with Moody over the matter and suggested some options for change. Moody misinterpreted her letter, inferred that she was being high-handed in her role, and responded tersely, offering his resignation and saying that "for six months I have had to oppose some of the dearest friends I have ever had, and I am tired and sick of it." Mrs. McCormick immediately offered her resignation if that would pacify Moody, knowing that his departure "would dissolve it [the society] at once." It was Emma, according to James Findlay, who "worked to restore order." As soon as she learned of the controversy, Emma wrote a long letter to Mrs. McCormick in an effort to mollify the situation. Moody then wired a telegram to Mrs. McCormick to smooth things over—probably at the insistence of Emma.[13]

In her ministry as a mother, Emma, like most Christian mothers of her era, saw it as her responsibility to train the children in religious matters.

> The teaching procedures she followed were time-honored. Each Sunday afternoon the children undertook the task of memorizing certain of the Psalms and selected passages from the Gospel narratives. As Emma's young charges bent to their duties she remained with them, seeking to answer questions and illuminate the meaning of passages as best she knew how. She was firm and unyielding in her demands that what seemed at the time a thankless job—to young Emma, Will, and Paul at least—was to be completed in its entirety.[14]

Emma's concern for the spiritual development of her children was also evident after they left home. When Will, whose devotion to the faith of his parents had begun to wane, went off to Yale in 1887, Emma wrote of her concern for his "being in any college without reliance on the help of Christ." She reminded him that "Papa I know is praying and I am that God's spirit may lead you to give up yourself to Christ entirely." Her exhortations did not end with that: "I don't believe my dear boy that anything else will really satisfy you. You know what you ought to do, then do it, not halfway but out and out. . . . It is not for dying alone but for right living you will need help stronger than you own."[15]

Emma's anxiety over Will's spiritual condition persisted, and two years later, while she was traveling with Moody, she wrote her son a detailed letter, cautioning him against becoming involved in worldly pleasures:

> We have in the West seen so much of young men, some that are noble young men & some that are wrecks. My thoughts have so often gone to you with the prayer also that you might be kept from sin. I know so much more about the temptations than if I had always lived quietly at home & as I have known in College you don't know how I have yearned after you & prayed that you might be kept. I have a horror of strong drink and its dreadful power but I have as great a dread of a sin that I know young men fall a victim to as often & now as I write I know you wont laugh or make light of my earnest prayer for you that you may be kept from the first steps either in drink or in impurity. You are not stronger than other men & temptations are ready. Don't depend on yourself but look to the same source for help in overcoming that we go to for you. May God keep & bless my dear boy![16]

During most of the Moodys' married life, Emma had no permanent residence to call her home. Many of her days and nights were spent in hotels or homes of strangers as she and Moody traveled in America and abroad. Only in her final years did she have a feeling of stability, when she lived in Moody's childhood home in Northfield, Massachusetts, which had been restored.[17]

The only time during their early married years that they were settled in a home for an extended time was when they were in Chicago. Their first home was a small cottage—"a cheery and hospitable home." "It was generally full of visitors, both old friends and strangers; and all the poor of the neighborhood soon learned the number on its door." The happy years in that cottage came to a sudden end when some of Moody's friends surprised the family with a rent-free "elegant" house, fully furnished. It was a dream come true, but their residence in that home was of short duration. In 1871 that home was destroyed by the great Chicago fire.[18]

The fire began on Sunday evening, October 8, while Moody was preaching to a packed audience at Farwell Hall. During the closing hymn they heard fire engine bells, and as soon as the service was over, it became evident that a major catastrophe was under way. Moody rushed home to rescue the family, and while he and Emma packed as many valuables as they could carry, they sent the children on ahead with a neighbor. Late that night they reached Emma's sister's suburban home to face the terrifying hours that lay ahead. "Throughout the next day the fire raged. Homeless thousands streamed out of the city, thieves looted, martial law was proclaimed, buildings were blown up to make a fire break. For twenty-four hours Dwight and Emma did not know whether their children had been trapped or saved."[19]

The family was reunited, and by Wednesday the fire was over. Two weeks later, their daughter Emma recalled, they made their way back "to the ruins of our house. Father went over everything in the ruins with a cane. The only thing of value he found was a toy iron stove of mine in perfect condition."[20]

Besides their home, both the mission school and church were burned to the ground, as were fifty other churches and missions. Moody appealed for aid from friends out East: "My plan is to raise $50,000 and put up a Tabernacle to accommodate seven or eight burnt out Missions."[21] His friends were generous, and the building was built, but Moody's ministry would no longer be confined to Chicago. The world became his mission field.

In 1873, the Moodys traveled to the British Isles, and that began the ministry they would have abroad in the years to follow. They had visited there earlier, but that was before he had teamed up with Ira D. Sankey, who brought inspiration to Moody's revival meetings through music. Almost from the beginning, Moody was attracting large crowds of hundreds of people. After three months in England, sometimes preaching at more than thirty meetings a week, the Moodys and Sankey went on to Scotland and Ireland

and then back to London, where, in 1875, Moody preached to crowds of nearly twenty thousand. After two years of virtually nonstop meetings, they returned to America; but there would be further trips abroad, and Moody "by 1880 was preaching in new and spacious Melbourne Hall, winning the favor of thousands of evangelicals across England and America."[22]

During Moody's hectic schedule in the British Isles, Emma served as his booking agent, among other things. He was often deluged with telegrams and messages pleading with him to fit just one more meeting into his already busy schedule, and it was Emma who juggled the time slots. In such circumstances, it would be natural if there had been marital strain, but that apparently was not the case. From Scotland she wrote to her mother, "Mr. Moody is nicer and kinder every day. He is a gem of a husband. I ought to be *very happy*."[23]

Emma had been involved in public ministry in the years before the children were born, but that quickly tapered off once the children came. She traveled abroad with her famous evangelist-husband, but frequently she stayed behind in London or someplace else while he preached. In 1883 she wrote to her mother from London that her husband was in Birmingham, while she and her teenage daughter "enjoy our quarters very much, and have quite pleasant times together" going to museums and seeing the sights of London.[24]

Although she was diagnosed by a physician as having a heart condition, Emma was well enough to travel and do considerable sight-seeing. Why, then, did she not accompany her husband and become active in public ministry like so many other pastors' wives? It was not because Moody objected to women's involvement in ministry. At a time when many preachers were outspoken in their objections to women's speaking publicly, Moody welcomed women into his circle of co-laborers. In 1877 he invited Frances Willard, the founder and president of the Women's Christian Temperance Union, to work in his Boston evangelistic campaign, which included preaching at the Sunday afternoon services. Likewise, Emma Dryer was a close associate; she directed Moody's Chicago Bible school ministry and helped to train Bible readers and city mission workers for more than fifteen years.[25] In light of this, Emma was noticeable in her absence from active public ministry.

Emma was often described as shy, and perhaps for her a public ministry would have been too strenuous. She strictly avoided any role that would put her in the limelight. According to her granddaughter, "she absolutely refused to appear on the platform in public meetings. 'Be conspicuous? Not she!' wrote her younger son."[26] From the beginning, Emma saw her primary ministry as that of helping her husband to be more effective in his public and private communication of the gospel, and in that effort she saw great success. At the time of Moody's death, a friend testified to the significant influence Emma had had on her husband: "In softening his asperities, . . . she polished his manners, she modified his brusqueness," and "taught him self-restraint."[27]

Emma's efforts to "remake" her husband were not a matter of resentment to Moody. Indeed, throughout his life he was conscious of his deficiencies, and he had the utmost confidence in his wife. Their son, Paul, who later became a Presbyterian minister and college president, wrote of the relationship between his parents and the deep respect his father had for his mother:

> My father's admiration for her was as boundless as his love for her. Till the day of his death he never ceased to wonder two things—the use God had made of him despite what he considered his handicaps, and the miracle of having won the love of a woman he considered so completely his superior. . . .
>
> To my mother, I am very sure, belongs the credit of having by precept and example made my father what he was in one respect, the most courteous man I ever knew.[28]

The genius of Emma as a wife was her ability to effect change in her husband without stifling his spirit. She was acutely aware of his raw potential, but at the same time conscious of his need for refinement. She believed in him and was his strongest and most loyal supporter, but she knew that her loyalty required that she also seek to check his weaknesses and capitalize on his strengths. According to their son, Moody "said that in the thirty-seven years of their married life she was the only one who had never tried to hold him back from anything he wanted to do and was always in sympathy with any new venture."[29]

DAISY SMITH

Daisy Smith
Forsaking Ministry for Marriage

Can a woman continue to have a meaningful ministry of her own after she marries a pastor? This is a difficult issue, and many women who have served in missionary work or some other kind of ministry have suddenly found their gifts for public ministry stifled as soon as they were married. Donna Sinclair writes about this: "When my husband was ordained, I cheerfully gave up my teaching career and set out with him to our first mission field. . . . So much for my career. I would spend my life assisting him in his." This initial experience was fulfilling for her, but as time went on, she became frustrated. "I was going to be the best minister's wife the world had ever seen. The house would be clean, the coffee on, and the Sunday school lessons prepared. . . . The major problem with this was an inevitable submergence of my identity into that of my husband."[1]

Donna's dissatisfaction was prompted to a great extent in that she was a capable woman with gifts of her own, but was repressed in her effort to be an individual in her own right. Her self-esteem, like that of many pastors' wives, was threatened by the fact that her identity had become too closely bound to her husband's.

In forsaking a ministry for marriage, many women have found themselves overwhelmed in domestic responsibilities while their husbands are engaged in a hectic ministry schedule. This is certainly not a problem limited to the modern age of technology, when workaholics are as common in the ministry as they are in corporate management. Margaret Baxter, wife of the renowned Puritan preacher Richard Baxter, struggled with this problem in the seventeenth century. Before they married, Baxter had made his position clear to his wife: "that she should expect none of my time which my ministerial work should require." This became a point of tension between them, and Baxter struggled with "whether to neglect his flock or his family" and with "guilt about omitting 'secret prayer with my wife when she desired it, for want of time, not daring to omit far greater work.'" He later concluded that, as far as ministers go, marriage ought "to be avoided as far as lawfully we may."[2]

One of the most missionary-oriented churches in the history of Christianity has been the People's Church in Toronto. The name associated with that church and that missionary vision is Oswald J. Smith; but alongside him stood a no less influential figure—Daisy Smith, whose zeal for missions went back to her early childhood and never abated throughout her long and fruitful life.

Daisy Billings was born in 1891 in Peterborough, Ontario. From her youth she was interested in foreign missions, and she made plans to attend Nyack Missionary College in New York for training. There were obstacles, however, that had to be overcome. Her father's meager income allowed no additional expense for her education, and in the first decade of the twentieth century, it was not the norm for a girl to go to college. Indeed, most of her friends had not even finished high school. But Daisy was determined, and during her last year of high school she found employment at the Peterborough Packaging Company. "The factory was one of those great medieval stone structures with a multitude of tiny, grimy windows, only a few of which opened. It had two great smokestacks belching black clouds of smoke defiantly into the hazy summer atmosphere hanging over Peterborough."[3]

After each pay period, Daisy went through the ritual of depositing her earnings at the local bank until she had reached her goal of sixty dollars—enough for travel and initial college fees. On arriving at campus in the fall of 1908, she was introduced to her roommate Adelaide—affectionately called "Ada"—who would become her dearest friend and partner in ministry. There were other friends as well, but Daisy was determined that her years of training would be devoted to education and ministry, not social life. Thus she was taken aback when she received a note from a friend one day while she was working in the school laundry. It was tucked inside his shirt pocket, where he knew she would see it:

Dear Miss Billings,

I have enjoyed our talks together so much. I get such a blessing whenever I hear you pray aloud in chapel. The more I get to know you the deeper my love for you grows. You are so tiny and dainty, and you have such a marvelous deep speaking voice. You are going to make a great preacher.

I think it is about time I told you I am falling in love with you.

Affectionately,
Dick Stanley

Daisy's response was characteristic of her philosophy toward her schooling and her goals for future ministry:

Dear Mr. Stanley,

I received your note that you sent me in the pocket of your shirt. I must tell you right away that I am not in love with anyone, and I don't want anyone to be in love with me just now. My only goal is to study God's Word, to be better equipped to preach it somewhere to those who have never heard. I have to devote all my time and energies to reaching my goal, and though I appreciate your kind thoughts of me, I am sure you will understand, and we shall continue to be good friends as we pray for each other.

In His service,
Daisy Billings[4]

It was during her final semester at Nyack that Daisy felt a specific call to the mission field. She and Ada had arrived in chapel late, and so concerned were they that they would be noticed and reported that they initially were sidetracked from the speaker—"a diminutive figure speaking in slow, deliberate tones, and barely visible behind the enormous pulpit." But from their back-row pew, Daisy and Ada were soon captivated by the woman's plaintive story about her work in Appalachia and the need for volunteers to come and reach out to these needy people with the gospel. Back in their dormitory room, Daisy and Ada prayed together. "They repeated the words of Adelaide's favorite hymn, 'Have Thine Own Way, Lord,' and knew God was calling them to minister to the neglected mountaineers of West Virginia."[5]

After completing their three-year course at Nyack, Daisy and Ada left the comforts of their culture to begin a tour of "foreign" missionary service in West Virginia. They were greeted at the train station by a burly miner in dirty overalls, who escorted them to their new home in Roaring Fork.

> Roaring Fork meant coal. Almost every adolescent and adult male worked in the mine. The miners' hours were long and life expectancies short. Life was generally cruel, marked by want of money, food, clothes, education—in short, want of all the things Ada and Daisy enjoyed from childhood. Contagious disease, particularly typhoid, spread almost unchecked and untreated, reaping its grim harvest. Families were generally large; children seemed to be everywhere as the wagon rolled along the dusty road, past rude cabins, dark and ominous, as if glowering at the awestruck missionaries.[6]

By the time the women arrived at their new home, it was getting dark, but it was still light enough for them to see that the tiny, run-down cabin had only two small windows and a dingy interior with "two rusty iron beds" that "sagged deeply under the weight of the lumpy mattresses." As soon as they were alone, they read and prayed together and then dropped exhausted into their beds—not realizing until morning that their beds were filled with bugs of varying description. In the morning their bodies were covered with bites and rashes.[7]

But there was no time for self-pity. Before they had time to investigate the premises, the two friends had a visitor—a woman whose grandson had died during the night. She had heard of the arrival of the preacher ladies, and she did not waste time in requesting their services. Daisy accompanied her to her run-down cabin, where she found the woman's daughter clutching the dead infant to her bosom. On seeing Daisy, the young mother handed the dead baby and some clothes to her and then left the house. It was a difficult initiation into missionary service, but Daisy had no choice but to dress the infant and prepare it for burial. The ceremony, conducted after the mother's return, was simple. After a brief time of prayer and Bible reading, Daisy comforted the mother and grandmother as best she could, then lowered the makeshift coffin into the ground. She could not doubt that she was where God wanted her to be in that moment in time and that her ministry was desperately needed.[8]

Soon after they arrived, Daisy and Ada announced they would be conducting Sunday services at the nearby, dilapidated schoolhouse. Ada played the old pump organ, and Daisy led the singing and delivered the sermon from behind her pulpit—an overturned ash can—to the handful of women and noisy children who came for the social atmosphere as much as the religious. The only man who showed any interest in spiritual matters was Joe, and one Sunday, to their amazement, he arrived with a group of tobacco-chewing miners. Joe stayed behind that day after the others filed out, and he made a profession of faith in Christ. In the months that followed, he eagerly attended services and, with the help of Daisy, learned to read so that he could study the Bible on his own. Without his telling her, she discovered that he "had begun to travel about Appalachia on foot, preaching wherever listeners would gather."[9]

Although it was a difficult ministry for Daisy and Ada, their labors were rewarded with the progress they witnessed as the months went by. But their stay in Roaring Fork came to a sudden end when Ada received news that her mother in Toronto was dying. Enclosed in the letter were two one-way tickets home, and the young women knew they had no choice but to relinquish their work to Joe and return home to fulfill family obligations.[10]

In Toronto, Daisy stayed in Ada's home to help during the trying months of Ada's bereavement. It was a period that offered time for reflection and contemplation about her life and her future goals—a time during which she made the decision to enroll in the deaconess training course of the Presbyterian Church of Canada. On completing the course, Daisy took an assignment to write a history of the Presbyterian deaconess movement, and it was this assignment that opened the door for ministry she could never have imagined or expected. She began receiving invitations to speak on the subject, and soon her reputation as a captivating speaker was widely recognized. "The importance of those early speaking engagements," writes her daughter, "was that God gave to her a recognition of her preaching gift."[11]

Daisy's flair for speaking soon caught the interest of J. D. Morrow, the eccentric and popular preacher of Dale Presbyterian Church. He invited her to join his staff, still in the capacity of a deaconess. They worked as a team, and it was not unusual for passersby to see him driving around Toronto on his canopy-covered motorcycle—his hair blowing in the wind—with Daisy riding behind him.[12]

This ministry was varied and interesting. Daisy served as a visitation pastor, conducted personal counseling, and spent many hours each week in relief work in the slums. She was particularly sensitive to the needs of new immigrants who could not speak English and were struggling to find adequate housing and employment. In her work as a deaconess, she joined the ranks of many other women who had sacrificially served in the inner cities. Indeed, some church leaders believed that the only way to save the ghettos from vice and corruption was to invade them with dedicated deaconesses. Christian Golder, writing in 1903, vividly described the saloons, the gambling and opium dens, and the houses of ill repute in the cities—and then offered his solution.

> More than ever before are we in need to-day of female power. We need women who will give up the luxuries of life, who will forsake society and friends, and condescend to help this class of men. . . . The only hope and possibility of elevating and saving this class of the population in our great cities lies in the unselfish and devoted activity of such women. . . . Here is the great and useful field for deaconesses. . . . The time will come when tens of thousands of deaconesses, in city and country, will sacrifice their lives in Christian love service.[13]

Work in the ghettos was considered valid "women's work," and Daisy found it fulfilling. But the ministry that she found most gratifying and for which she felt most gifted was preaching. Morrow encouraged her in this regard and set aside one Sunday evening each month for her to preach to the congregation. "The people responded in tears and laughter, in thanksgiving and service. These months of regular preaching left little doubt in her mind—preaching was her forte." Daisy was convinced that "at last God had demonstrated the power of the gift he had bestowed on her. She was to be a preacher."[14]

Daisy's prominence as Morrow's assistant suddenly came to a halt in 1915, when Morrow announced that he had decided to hire an associate pastor. Although Daisy had essentially fulfilled that role, she was technically a deaconess. The change would mean her preaching ministry would be curtailed, as would other "associate pastor" duties that she had fulfilled. She was openly hostile about the turn of events, and when Oswald J. Smith, the new pastor arrived, she did not go out of her way to make him feel welcome. Within months, however, Oswald was writing of his growing attachment for her in his diary, and he was seriously contemplating her as a life partner. He did not take the matter of marriage lightly, as his personal reflections indicate:

> I would value more, and rather have, a woman's love than all the fame that the whole world could heap upon me. *Souls come first,* but the next great craving of my heart is the yearning for a helpmeet. God grant that she may rise to my largeness of vision, with an understanding of the great ambition of my heart.[15]

In the late summer of 1916, when both were in their mid-twenties, Oswald and Daisy were married. The decision had not been easy for Daisy. She considered herself a professional. She was fully as capable of pastoral ministry as Oswald. Marriage would mean relinquishing much that she had longed for, because "no married woman went on with her work in those days."[16]

Daisy was not the first woman Oswald had loved. There had been Jennie before her. Jennie was a nurse whom Oswald met during his student days at Toronto Bible College. When he went out on preaching assignments, she often went with him and sang. It was "one of the sweetest, one of the most sacred experiences of my life," he later wrote. They became engaged, but two years later she began to have doubts when he was in Chicago studying at McCormick Theological Seminary; while he was involved in a summer ministry in Kentucky, she broke the news to him.

It was a distressing time for Oswald. "Only God knows the sorrow and heartache, the bitter, bitter disappointment, the days of suffering and suspense," he later wrote. He referred to the experience as "the greatest sorrow of my life." But he refused to give up all hope. On July 12, 1915, back in Toronto, Oswald took Jennie canoeing. She could not be persuaded to change her mind, and it was their final time together. Less than a year later, Oswald became engaged to Daisy, and soon after—some might say on the rebound from Jennie—he married her.[17]

Daisy's initiation into the job of pastor's wife came very quickly after they were married. Morrow took a leave of absence from the church, and Oswald was named acting pastor. But almost immediately, his evangelical fervor clashed with the staid Presbyterian formality entrenched in the church. People were shocked when he hung a banner with red lettering, GET RIGHT WITH GOD, in the front of the sanctuary. There were also objections to the type of gospel music he insisted be sung in congregational and choir numbers. The infighting finally culminated with the resignation of the choir director and the senior elder. The "first four months at the helm had indeed been stormy ones, and again the battle took its toll: Oswald could not sleep, and his head throbbed and ached all night. Utterly exhausted and unable to carry on with the work, he took a month's leave of absence."[18]

On returning to his post at the Dale Presbyterian Church, Oswald began praying for revival with others who were in sympathy with his vision. This "Soul-saving Gang," as they were dubbed, did not include any of the church's elders, and the tension that was so evident earlier did not diminish.

It was a difficult time for Daisy. When she married Oswald, the newspaper article had carried the headline "Assistant Pastor of New Dale Presbyterian Church Weds Its Popular Deaconess." She had been deeply loved by the people, and now, as the pastor's wife, she found herself in the middle of bitter controversy. She herself was concerned that the ongoing work of the church was being neglected because of the time Oswald spent in praying for revival. There were other sore points. She "was smarting, in spite of her adoration for her new husband. Not only had Oswald never asked her to preach, keeping the pulpit for himself, but also what had happened to those dreams she and Oswald had shared of lovely evenings together in their own little parlor?" Oswald's revival prayer meetings and church activities sometimes kept him away from home from before dawn until late at night.[19]

The situation came to a climax when Morrow returned from his leave of absence in 1918. He was not happy with the changes Oswald had made, and he publicly accused Oswald of having increased the indebtedness of the church. As a result, Oswald resigned and the board, to his "stunned sorrow," accepted it—thus ending three and a half stormy years of ministry there. He was out of work, and there was now a baby adding to their financial burdens, requiring them to give up their apartment and move in with Daisy's parents.[20]

The next year, with no other options for ministry, Oswald and Daisy packed their belongings and their little one and headed for British Columbia to do mission work among the lumberjacks. Whether Daisy had misgivings about her marriage is not recorded, but she was not happy.

> It turned out to be a miserable spring and summer for Daisy. Moving five times in the first three months—from damp basements and single rooms before settling into a fairly comfortable furnished home at Kitsalano Beach—did not help her. Oswald was away most of the time for periods of three to four days or a week. . . . When he was home, he was busy correcting the proofs for a poetry manuscript. . . .
>
> In his absence, Daisy did some speaking, and often visited with two Presbyterian deaconess friends she had come to know during her training in Toronto. But most of the time she felt wretched: she was pregnant again and Glen [the baby] had been seriously ill, but most of the misery was in her own soul.[21]

After some months in Western Canada, Oswald decided to return to Toronto, where once again they lived with Daisy's parents and where their second child was born. Again Oswald began traveling with short-term ministries, and "once again Daisy was in torment, hating the separation. Now she began to think that Oswald no longer loved her and just wanted to get away from her, or that maybe God was punishing her for not being a good enough wife. . . ." The little ones suffered, too. Daisy reported that Glen commented, "I have no Daddy to love me." There were physical discomforts as well, the family often going without meals for lack of money.[22]

In 1920, at the age of thirty-one, Oswald was still struggling with his conviction that God had a mighty ministry for him. Yet the doors all seemed to be closed. For a time he felt certain that he would be called to the pastorate of a Baptist church, but that opportunity was given to another. It was in this gloomy state of affairs that he returned to Toronto and announced that he planned to rent the Royal Templar Hall, distribute handbills, and begin church services.

It. seemed like an outrageous decision—with rent alone costing twenty-five dollars a week—but Oswald would not be deterred. Fewer than one hundred came on the first Sunday, and the offering was less than six dollars, but Oswald refused to give up. Attendance and offerings grew, and after a few months he made arrangements to merge his congregation with a struggling church, Parkdale Tabernacle.[23]

With that merger and Oswald's initiation of tent meetings, his success in ministry suddenly began to turn around. Within a year, the congregation was outgrowing its facilities, and a new church building was under construction. As the congregation grew and the outreach expanded, the pastoral duties increased; but Oswald still found it difficult to stay in one place. "Calls began to come from various parts of the United States and Canada," he wrote in his autobiography, "and from that time I started leaving Toronto and my work to hold special meetings in other places."

In 1924, leaving Daisy and the three little ones behind, Oswald went to Europe and Russia to hold special evangelistic meetings. In 1926, amid problems and dissension, he resigned from the Alliance Tabernacle in Toronto, and as in the case of Dale Presbyterian Church, "was stricken dumfounded and unbelieving" when his resignation was accepted. He spent much of the next two years traveling.[24]

Daisy was pleased with the recognition accorded her husband, but she often felt overwhelmed when she was left alone for weeks and months on end with three small children. Baby Paul suffered from violent seizures, and only a mother alone with a feverish child in the middle of the night can identify with the terror and fear of death that such convulsions elicit. She was depressed and overcome with insecurities, as her words to her husband indicate:

Why, O, why is God taking you away from me when you are more to me than words can ever express? I only wish I were worthy of you and filled in your life the way I ought to. I fall so short of my own ideal for myself as wife and mother, and often wish, really and truly, that I were taken away so that before you are old you might have a more ideal woman.[25]

It is difficult to imagine Daisy, who had been so effective in ministry before she was married, wishing she were dead. Like so many educated and gifted women before and after her, however, her self-esteem plummeted after she married. From God she had received a high calling—Christian ministry—but because she was a woman, that calling had been thwarted. Her husband's calling superceded hers, and she was forced to bury her gifts and shoulder the responsibilities of the family. She "had to learn how to manage everything concerned with the house as if she were a widow," her daughter later wrote. "Replacing a blown fuse or repairing any household item was foreign to him." When he was home, she made sure she kept "the children from his study door . . . so that they would not disturb him."[26]

Oswald was not entirely oblivious to her pain. On the first leg of his six-month journey to Russia, he wrote her a sentimental poem—perhaps to somehow assuage his guilt:

Did you break your heart today
Ere you tore yourself away
When you knew I could not stay?

I am brokenhearted too,
For I long so much for you
And I know not what to do.

When I saw the teardrops start,
I would clasp you to my heart,
Never from you would I part.

How my heart goes out to you
For I know you suffer too,
And your love is strong and true.[27]

Despite her despair over Oswald's frequent and long departures, Daisy went on with her life and effectively ministered in her capacity as a pastor's wife. She taught a woman's Bible class at church and was involved in a variety of other church ministries, including counseling. On the very night that Oswald left for Russia, she received a call for him at midnight from a desperate woman, confined to a wheelchair, whose drunken husband had beaten her and locked her in a room and left the house. Daisy called the police and accompanied them to the woman's house. By the time they arrived, the husband had returned home. After the police left, Daisy talked with the couple at length, and through her counsel the husband professed faith in Christ.[28]

In 1927 Oswald accepted a call to the pastorate of a church in Los Angeles. He and Daisy and the children traveled by train, but no sooner had they arrived than Oswald was certain he had made a wrong choice. He called back to Toronto to stop the furniture movers, only to find they had already left on the journey. Again Daisy was devastated. Oswald agreed to stay a year despite his misgivings. His ministry saw success, but after exactly one year he resigned and returned to Toronto, hoping to resume his ministry at his old church. He was permitted to preach one Sunday, "but he would not be allowed back in. Finally, after two years, that was made irrevocably clear to Oswald. The work was lost to him forever."[29]

After doing further itinerant evangelistic work, Oswald returned to Toronto once again to begin a new church. He was approaching forty, and he offered his services to Paul Rader, the president of Worldwide Christian Couriers, to begin an evangelistic center in Toronto. Oswald was widely known, so when he returned to speak at Massey Hall, he attracted large crowds, and out of that effort, the Peoples Church was founded. Finally, after so many stops and starts, Oswald was settling into a long-term ministry. He would remain pastor of that church for some thirty years. But even then he was away for long periods of time. He still felt burned from the rejection by his previous church: "For some time I did not take much interest in the work. . . . Very often I left others in charge and travelled all over the United States holding campaigns."[30]

In less than a year after he had founded the Peoples Church, Oswald went abroad to make a tour of Russian and Spanish mission fields. "I need you, and the children need you," Daisy pleaded, for she was, as one writer states, "stung by his excitement, even eagerness, to leave her for the anticipated missionary journey." Again she felt abandoned, and her self-esteem was jarred. A letter addressed to him in Berlin revealed her anguish and self-doubt: "Perhaps God is punishing me for not being the wife I should have been to you. I sometimes get thinking of heaven where you will be so far above me that I will never see you, and it depresses me so." It was a pitiful confession of a middle-aged woman. Her next lines poignantly reveal her state of mind: "I try to be brave, but I feel so defeated by it all."[31]

Oswald returned from abroad several months later. "For two days the family had him to themselves while he organized his slides," but within two weeks he had left for speaking engagements in Chicago, Minneapolis, Dallas, and on the West Coast. He always returned to Toronto—to the Peoples Church and to Daisy—but in the years that followed, world travel almost became a way of life.[32]

As much as Daisy had despaired over her husband's frequent departures, it was a way of life that she had become used to. She was a devoted mother, and she knew that her children desperately needed at least one parent on whom they could depend. It was not out of character for her, then, that when Oswald invited her to join him in world travel, she turned the offer down. "You never wanted me with you before, and I'm not going now. The children still need me." They ranged in ages from sixteen to twenty-one, and Oswald believed they were old enough to stay alone, but Daisy adamantly refused. "All his protests were in vain. He and Daisy quarreled, and Oswald left, feeling deeply hurt, thinking that Daisy was putting the children ahead of him." She was not without guilt over this incident—especially after she received a cable from Australia saying that her husband was seriously ill.[33]

The day did arrive when Daisy felt she could leave the children behind and travel with her husband. But she traveled as a companion, not as a minister in her own right. Yet she made the most of her opportunities, and when she returned home to Canada, she sought opportunities to speak to women's groups on the needs of women overseas. One such opportunity came from the World Literature Crusade in California. She was invited to do a one-month's series of radio and television programs. It was a grand occasion for her once again to use her gifts and abilities in a mighty way. She gave graphic accounts of the dire circumstances of women in many of the countries she had visited and appealed for help from American women on behalf of their sisters overseas.[34]

In later years, Daisy's health did not always permit her to travel, but by the time she reached eighty she had accompanied Oswald on nine overseas trips. After that there would be no more trips abroad. She died in her early eighties in 1972.[35]

Was Daisy's sacrifice worth the price? Did she bury her gifts for so many years for nothing? She would have said that the price she paid was worth it all. One of her deepest joys was seeing her youngest son, Paul, enter the ministry and succeed his father as the senior pastor at Peoples Church. She knew that her years of sacrifice had not been for naught, but she knew too that the cost had been high. She was a highly gifted woman, and one can only wonder to what extent God might have used her had her marriage to Oswald been a full partnership in ministry.

CATHERINE MARSHALL

· 12 ·
Catherine Marshall
Standing in the Shadow
of a Superstar

One of the difficult struggles for many pastors' wives is having always to be in the shadow of a prominent husband. The pastor, by the nature of his work, is conspicuous in the parish work and often in the community. His wife, despite her own talents and abilities, sometimes goes unnoticed. This frustration is expressed by a woman who found that the creative gifts she offered to the church when she was single were no longer sought after once she became a pastor's wife: "I view my role in the church as a crippling suit of armor—unhealthy for me and vastly wasteful for the church. What I would like, and am working toward, is to be a free and creative lay woman, a helper to my husband, surely, but not a shadow that walks silently in his footsteps."[1]

According to Denise Turner, "Lots of ministers' wives also resent being thought of as female clones of their minister husbands. 'I'm never recognized unless I'm in the company of my husband,' numbers of them insist, 'and I got higher grades than he did in graduate school.' "[2]

How can a pastor affirm his wife when she is feeling the sting of nonrecognition? "I think it's great," writes Frances Nordland, "if a husband rejoices in his wife's talents and capabilities." Her own husband, in her words, "has enough 'on the ball' so that he doesn't need to keep his wife in the background. A man who is sure of himself and his own capabilities doesn't fear letting his wife develop and use her talents."[3]

For some women, the highest privilege they could dream of would be marriage to a popular, widely acclaimed minister of the gospel—a man who can stir the hearts of his parishioners as he stands behind the pulpit, while she uplifts him in prayer from her place in the pew. Her husband's glory would be hers, and she would always have the satisfaction that after all the accolades were over, when the door of the parsonage closed, he belonged to her.

That romantic scenario seldom becomes reality, however. It is true that the women share in the joy that comes with seeing their husbands' ministries flourish. But they also encounter loneliness and isolation that is often magnified by their husbands' success. Many women since Katie Luther have been married to superstars in the pulpit and have experienced all these feelings. Catherine Marshall is a noteworthy example.

Unlike most wives of superstar pastors, Catherine did not struggle over many years in attaining that status. Unlike Eunice Beecher and Daisy Smith, whose husbands had relatively small and difficult pastorates in their early years, Catherine married Peter Marshall when he was already the pastor of a large church in Atlanta. His reputation for stirring sermons was widely known, and he was, in the minds of many, on the make as one of America's great preachers. When they wed, Peter was thirty-five and Catherine, twenty-two.

Catherine Wood grew up in the South in the 1920s. Her father was a Presbyterian minister who served parishes in Tennessee, Mississippi, and West Virginia. Religion played an important role in her early life. At age ten she was emotionally caught up by the spirit of revival when Gypsy Smith came to Canton, Mississippi, to hold tent meetings; soon after that, when her father gave an "invitation" at the close of the morning service, she went forward and, making her profession of faith, joined the church. It was not until her college years that she realized something was missing spiritually in her life. In her journal she wrote, "My religion is not on a very firm basis, I'm afraid. I have had no vital experience. God doesn't seem real to me." Little changed in the years that followed, and as a young preacher's wife, she continued to flounder spiritually. It was not until 1944, after a prolonged illness, that she could say she truly had a deep, experiential faith.[4]

Catherine was a student at Agnes Scott College when she became acquainted with Peter. She had heard him preach at the Westminster Presbyterian Church. For two years she "had longed to know this young Scotsman," but knew that he was heavily involved in his growing church. Besides, he was considered one of the most eligible bachelors in Atlanta, and what chance did she have among so many other young women who wanted to get to know him better? To her parents, who were familiar with his preaching, she wrote, "Mr. Marshall conducts beautiful services, and I like him more each time I go. . . . I have never heard such prayers in my life. It's as if, when he opens his mouth, there is a connected line between you and God. I know this sounds silly, but I've got to meet that man. . . ."[5]

Like a fairy-tale romance, Catherine and Peter did become acquainted with each other, and after a number of casual encounters, their paths crossed again when they happened to be involved at the same church function. They talked and enjoyed each other's company, and "six dates, four chaperons, and a dozen months later," they became engaged.[6] Catherine recorded in her journal the times they shared leading up to that momentous occasion: "Peter was terribly solicitous about my illness. . . . I believe now he wants to be serious. . . . I think Peter is in love with me!! . . . Tonight we went to a play. Afterwards on the front porch he kissed me again and again. . . . Tonight we talked until three in the morning and he proposed. . . ."[7]

For a woman barely past the age of twenty, the prospects of marriage to this celebrity preacher was an exhilarating episode in her life—coming at the very end of her college days. She knew she was the envy of other single women in the church, and her life seemed to float on the fantasy of the idyllic life as the wife of this illustrious preacher. She was not unaware of his popularity with women: "There was a period when the mothers of Atlanta debutantes, no less than the daughters, considered him very eligible husband material and were on his trail. . . . Peter was a man's man. Yet he was the target for much feminine admiration."[8]

So busy was Peter with his church and speaking engagements

elsewhere that it was difficult to schedule a wedding date. And hardly was the wedding over when Peter was called to candidate at the prestigious New York Avenue Presbyterian Church in Washington, D.C., with some twelve hundred members. It had been President Lincoln's church during the Civil War, and many well-known politicians and bureaucrats were on its membership rolls. The call was extended to Peter, but he turned it down because he believed his leaving would be detrimental to the Atlanta church. A second call was extended, and he agreed to accept, but insisted that he delay his coming for nearly a year. The congregation considered his coming worth waiting for, and in 1937 the Marshalls moved to Washington.[9]

Peter was quickly drawing overflow crowds—large enough to capture the attention of journalists who reported that an average of five hundred people were turned away from the service each Sunday. Only three months after he began his ministry, he was selected by the Washington Federation of Churches to preach at the joint Christmas service that would be attended by President Roosevelt and his family. The headlines in the *Baltimore Sun* the day afterward summed up the message with "Roosevelt Hears Sermon Assailing Mockery of War." The *Atlanta Journal* also reported the story, referring to Peter as "a preacher who was a favorite among Atlantans a short time ago." Newspapers all over the country carried the news of the celebrated young pastor.[10]

Amid all this adulation Catherine sought to find her niche as a pastor's wife. She was naturally shy, and the task before her was frightening. "At only 23 the young girl who had fled up the back stairs to avoid involvement with people now had to be hostess to a steady stream of social functions in one of Washington's largest downtown churches."[11] She quickly discovered that the expectations for that role were far higher than she could fulfill. It was simply assumed that the multi-talented, celebrated pastor should have an equally capable wife.

> New York Avenue expected a great deal of its minister's wife. To say that the pastor's helpmate was expected to be gracious, charming, poised, equal to every occasion, would be a gross understatement. She should be able to meet the most undistinguished or the most famous persons with equanimity. She should

know how to entertain two or two hundred. When called upon unexpectedly to a banquet or other church gathering, she should know how to speak well—entertainingly or inspiringly, as the occasion demanded. She was presumed to be the diplomat supreme. And she needed especially an unfailing sense of humor.[12]

Besides having such talents and gifts that would be easily observed in public, the pastor's wife was to model a deep spirituality, "to have much firsthand experience in the art of prayer," and "to love other people deeply and genuinely." But while modeling the ultimate in spiritual maturity, she "was to dress becomingly and to be as attractive as possible," so that the people could "be proud of *their* possession." "No wonder I felt inadequate," Catherine wrote. "I could, by no means, measure up to such a standard. God had to make many painful changes in me before I even began to measure up." She did, however, win their approval when she arrived one winter Sunday wearing a "fuchsia-colored hat" that had been purchased at "one of Connecticut Avenue's most expensive shops."[13]

If finding her proper role as a pastor's wife was confusing and frustrating, Catherine's role as the wife of Peter was clear-cut. He had strong convictions on a woman's place in the home, and Catherine willingly accepted his prescribed standard. "Keepers of the Springs," according to Catherine, was "probably the most popular sermon Peter ever preached. . . . Thousands of copies of it were sold in pamphlet form . . . mostly to women." The sermon was believed so significant by the *Washington Post* that an article appeared with the headline "Marriage a Full-Time Job for Any Woman, Asserts Pastor." The article quoted Peter's criticism of the current lifestyle that was emerging—especially in Washington, a career-oriented city.

> "Many girls today are unwilling to make marriage a full-time job. . . . The idea of a woman's taking time out from business to start a family is not only absurd, but it is breaking down the fundamental ideals of family life."

The article further summarized his views: "Women's greatest chance for making marriage a success depends upon her willingness to lose her life in that of her husband, Dr. Marshall holds.

He means that the wife's interests must be those of her husband."[14]

Catherine's interests were those of Peter's. During her twelve years of marriage, she wrote, "I had stayed in the background—a behind-the-scenes wife." Indeed, so far behind the scenes "that there were those in my husband's congregation who did not know whether or not the minister was married, or at best, had never seen me." This, according to Catherine, "was quite in keeping with Peter's ideas and ideals on the subject of marriage." It was Catherine who made this restrictive view of marriage work. "There might well have been some conflict between Peter and me over his strong views on the role of women in marriage had I not discovered early in our life together that putting these ideas into practice brought me joy and satisfaction at a deep level."[15]

Although Catherine willingly accepted her role as a pastor's wife and homemaker, she became very frustrated during her early years at New York Avenue Presbyterian Church. Like Daisy Smith, she was overshadowed by her larger-than-life husband, and her sense of self-worth crumbled. "It seemed to me that Peter was altogether capable of carrying the responsibility of his ministry with no help from me." Peter's independent lifestyle only served to aggravate Catherine's self-doubts. Before he was married "he had fallen into the habit of keeping all-day office hours in his study at the church. Neither did he take a day off each week. . . . At night he usually had a meeting or speaking engagements," and sometimes he was out of town for days at a time for special meetings. He saw no reason to change his schedule after he was married, and thus Catherine faced many lonely hours. To complicate matters, Peter, who had "difficulty in expressing his deepest feelings," did "not easily open his heart and mind" to her.[16]

When Peter did arrive home after a long day at his study, he could be sharp and critical. One night when Catherine had prepared a meal that he did not find appealing, "a look of undisguised disgust crossed his face as he sat down and folded his napkin." Then, with no apparent feeling of guilt, considering the effort she had made in cooking the meal, he said: "Catherine, I guess you'll have to ask the blessing tonight. God knows I'm not grateful for turkey hash, and I can't fool Him."[17]

Catherine's struggles as a pastor's wife involved not only her own inadequacies and feelings of isolation, but also the conflicts her husband faced in a large city church. Despite his celebrity status, Peter was not without opposition when he sought to introduce change. Most of the trustees were very cautious regarding financial matters, and they strongly objected to his plans for expansion. And like pastors of far less fame, he suffered from the little aggravations. Once when he forgot to send a sympathy note to a church member whose mother had died, he was detained after the church service and given "a prolonged verbal spanking." So, while she enjoyed the acclaim her husband received, Catherine also suffered with him when parish problems arose.[18]

Peter's fame as the most popular preacher in the nation's capital did not go unnoticed by politicians, and in 1947 he was elected the chaplain of the United States Senate. This high honor, however, was marred by the political infighting that accompanied the decision. That post had been typically considered nonpolitical, and when the opposition party acquired a majority, the position was not influenced by party loyalties. But in 1947 some members of the newly installed Republican majority wanted Peter to replace Dr. Harris, the pastor of Washington's Foundry Methodist Church. "All of this was very painful to Peter," Catherine wrote, but he accepted the post, and quickly gained the respect of the Senate as a whole. In fact, two years later, he was "unanimously reelected by the Democrats." Subsequently he had the privilege of taking part in the Inauguration Day ceremonies of President Harry Truman.[19]

Five days after she had witnessed the inauguration, Catherine received a phone call from the hospital telling her that Peter was dead. Her life—her whole existence—had revolved around her husband, and now he was gone. She was left alone with nine-year-old Peter John, utterly unprepared to manage her life without the man on whom she had so completely depended.[20]

The massive coronary that took Peter's life in 1949, when he was only forty-six, was not the first sign of heart disease. He had previously suffered a heart attack, but he continued his hectic pace despite advice from his physician that he lighten his work load. Catherine desperately tried to reason with him, to little avail. "As out-of-town speaking engagements piled up, I battled my increasing fear for Peter. The second year after his attack, he had made ten such trips; the next year, it had been twenty. And all had been sandwiched in between a constant round of in-town duties, talks, and appearances." Finally Catherine's anxiety reached the point where she knew she had to do something. If she could not change her husband, she would change herself. "Nothing seemed left for me but a complete relinquishment of the man I loved to his Lord." She told Peter of her changed attitude. "He was happy to have an end to the conflict between us."[21]

Deep down, Catherine feared that the celebrity status of her husband that she so enjoyed and was so proud of would be the very thing to take him from her. But all the fears and premonitions in the world could not have prepared her for the inevitable. Words could not express the numbing grief she suffered, especially during those first weeks and months of widowhood. She faced the various stages of the grief process—at first denying that it was true, and then, eight days after the funeral, realizing "with full certainty that Peter's death was real—final. There would be no reprieve from that cruel fact."

On accepting that reality, Catherine began to suffer from guilt, blaming herself for little things that could not be changed. She hated herself for having snapped at Peter about his planned trip that would have taken him away over Valentine's Day—after he had lightheartedly asked her if she would be his valentine. She could never undo that remark, and the guilt welled up inside her. But if she was angry with herself, she was even angrier with God. "If God is a God of love and has the power to help us, why didn't he do something about Peter's heart?"[22]

As the weeks wore on, Catherine quickly discovered that there was more than grief to cope with. Few women could have been less prepared for independence than she. "In many ways, I was still a little girl. I had adored and leaned on my husband. . . . I had never once figured out an income tax blank, had a car inspected, consulted a lawyer, or tried to read an insurance policy." These were not the kinds of things that Peter believed ought to concern a housewife. To complicate matters, Peter had not left a will, which meant that, according to District of Columbia statutes, two-thirds of the estate would be placed in trust for young Peter, and Catherine would receive only a third. Even her son's guardianship had to be established in court.[23]

That the widow of a nationally known, superstar pastor would face unconsoling grief at his death might be expected, but that she would face poverty was the last thought that would enter people's minds. Yet it was a grave reality for Catherine. There was no life insurance and only a small pension of less than two hundred dollars a month from the Presbyterian Ministers Fund—not nearly enough for Catherine and her son to live on in the Washington area. She was advised immediately to sell the car and their Cape Cod cottage just so she and her son could survive until she found a way to earn a living. But Peter had never felt it was necessary for a married woman to be able to support herself, and Catherine, having married before she received a teaching certificate, was skeptical. She had no secretarial skills or other abilities that would be sought after in the job market.[24]

It was the suggestion of a friend that launched Catherine into an independent life that would lead to celebrity status in her own right. Why not publish Peter's sermons? To Catherine, this suggestion involved far more than the possibility of earning some desperately needed money. It would be a way for her to help keep her husband's memory alive. She worked feverishly on the project and in late November, less than a year after Peter died, the book was on the market. *Mr. Jones, Meet the Master* (the title taken from one of Peter's sermons) was an immediate success. Within months, tens of thousands of copies had been sold.[25]

The dream of one day being a writer was something Catherine had fanaticized about since childhood. Yet without her marriage to a celebrated preacher and without his tragic and premature death, that dream may never have been fulfilled.

Peter's life and ministry became the focus of Catherine's early writings. She published a volume of his prayers and then his biography, *A Man Called Peter,* which, next to the Bible, was the nation's best-selling book in 1952 and was made into a movie by Twentieth-Century Fox. Other books followed soon after, detailing the trials of Catherine's widowhood and her quest for spiritual maturity in the years subsequent to Peter's death. She would write many more books and would become one of the most celebrated

Christian authors of the mid-twentieth century—far excelling her husband's fame while he was alive.

In 1959 Catherine married Leonard LeSourd, who had three school-age children of his own and was the editor of *Guideposts* magazine. It was a change in lifestyle to be the stepmother of three school-age children, and there was a change of environment. They all lived together in a "sprawling white house with red shutters . . . set in the rocky, tree-shaded countryside of Westchester County."[26] But it was a happy life for Catherine and Leonard. Their interests and writing careers meshed well, and he strongly encouraged her to be her own person. His concept of the role of a wife was far different from Peter's. With Leonard's approval, Catherine retained the name "Marshall" for professional use. This meant that LeSourd was often perceived as "Mr. Catherine Marshall," but he accepted that role. In Catherine's words, "There was no masculine ego involved."[27]

During her twenty-three years of marriage to LeSourd, Catherine wrote some of her most widely read books, including the novel *Christy* and the nonfictional *Beyond Our Selves, Something More, The Helper,* and *Meeting God at Every Turn.* When Catherine died in 1983 at the age of sixty-eight, her husband spoke of the "rare opportunity and privilege to have those 23 years." They had shared much in their combined careers of writing and had benefited by it: "We would talk about characters and plot. We'd argue and struggle. I loved it; she was so intense, always testing our beliefs and convictions."[28]

One can only wonder what Peter Marshall would have thought of his wife's celebrity status. Since his death she had come out from behind his clerical robes and had demonstrated to herself and to the world that she had gifts that far surpassed those necessary for being a behind-the-scenes wife. She had been happy standing in his shadow, but after she was forced to step out alone she discovered how powerful her own ministry (and her husband's) could be through her pen. Many people wrote that they had never heard of Peter Marshall until her books were published.

But far more than fame was involved in Catherine's writing. She wrote first and foremost to minister to needy people. As a pastor's wife she touched the hearts of many, including pastors' wives who would live out their days in relative obscurity. After *A*

Man Called Peter was published, Catherine received a letter from a pastor's wife in a rural Iowa town whose marriage had turned sour after her two little ones came along and difficulties arose in the church. The situation had reached a boiling point on New Year's Eve, when their baby-sitter was unable to come and she had to stay home from the party and watch-night service. While she was alone after the children were in bed, her eyes fell on a book she received as a Christmas gift—*A Man Called Peter*. In her letter to Catherine this distressed mother said, "Somehow reading your book, something in me melted. . . . In those hours I grew up. That night Dennis and I knelt down together and with unashamed tears turned it all over to God and started a fresh chapter in our marriage."[29] This is just one example of how the story of one struggling pastor's wife strengthened another struggling pastor's wife.

RUTH PEALE

· 13 ·
Ruth Peale
Deflecting Discouragement
With Positive Thinking

Some of the greatest spiritual giants in the history of the church have suffered from deep depression. It was true of the pioneer missionary to Burma, Adoniram Judson, and it was true of the great pastor and missionary statesman A. B. Simpson. It is often the wife's task to maintain an equilibrium in the home to bring her husband out of his gloomy despair.

Ruth Senter recognizes depression as a potential problem in clergy marriages. In one of her books she devotes a chapter to "Life—a Pain or a Pleasure? Learning about Positive Outlooks." Here she quotes Proverbs 15:15: "When a man is gloomy, everything seems to go wrong. When he is cheerful, everything seems right." She emphasizes the importance of the pastor's wife's attitude: "An interesting thing about the climate of my life is that it's contagious. Happiness is catching. So is gloom. If I am not a happy person to be around, there is a good possibility that those around me won't be happy either."[1]

Frances Nordland admonishes pastors' wives to take precautions if their husbands show signs of depression or nervous exhaustion: "if you notice that he angers too quickly, laughs nervously, or cannot control his emotions when he's preaching. These are signs that he's in danger of an emotional explosion."

Besides obvious remedies such as taking a day off each week for relaxation, she counsels the wife to have a positive attitude and to meet her "husband's emotional needs by a warm response to his demonstrations of affection" and by "sympathetic understanding."[2]

Betty Coble addresses the problem of a pastor's wife dealing with a hurting husband, and she acknowledges that frequently "the wife may become frustrated because she is not able to lift his burden or relieve his pain." But Coble encourages the wife not to become overwhelmed with despondency. "She is privileged to share the real person he is and know how to pray for him intelligently. She can ask for God's wisdom to see the needs she can meet in his life—such as always listening to him. She may be able to provide a fresh viewpoint."[3] Not all women are able to meet their husband's needs effectively in this way, but some have done so superbly, and Ruth Peale is an example.

Norman Vincent Peale has often been thought of as the most optimistic man in America. His book *The Power of Positive Thinking* has sold millions of copies since its publication in 1952, and his radio and television programs have reflected the same theme of attaining new spiritual heights and achieving success in everyday life through positive thinking. But behind the scenes, Norman Vincent Peale has struggled with discouragement; the optimism that he so often lacked was supplied by his wife Ruth, who put positive thinking into daily practice in the home and in their ministry.

Ruth Stafford was born into a Methodist preacher's family in rural Iowa. It was a musical family, and in some Methodist circles they became known as the "singing Staffords." "Religion was a part of our life," Ruth recalls, "but it was not a self-conscious or ultra-pious religion. It was something to be lived, not talked about at length. We said grace at meals. Sunday was a quiet day—no movies, no noisy games. From the start, my own faith seemed as natural as breathing."[4]

After graduating from a Detroit high school at the age of sixteen, Ruth enrolled at a local city college. Her education was interrupted after one year, however, when her parents decided she should drop out and work in order to finance her older brother's final year of college at Syracuse University. He would, in turn, help her financially with her education when he was able to do so. It was a distressing time for her. Ruth had thoroughly enjoyed her first year of college and was frustrated that at seventeen she was being asked to forego her plans temporarily in favor of her brother. By the time she returned, her friends would be a year ahead of her and involved in new interests. She stoically agreed to the plan, never dreaming how significantly it would affect her future.[5]

Ruth later realized that God had destined the decision for her to remain out of school that year. When she did return to college, she followed her brother's footsteps to Syracuse. There in 1927, during her senior year, Norman Peale, a young pastor who had already served in two other Methodist churches, began his ministry at the University Church. Had she not relinquished her own education to help finance her brother's by working at a telephone company, she never would have met him. She would have graduated before he arrived on the scene.[6]

Ruth had heard about Norman from her sorority sisters before she met him. They were impressed by his good looks and charm and by the fact that he was single. For Norman, none of these girls had caught his attention, but his meeting Ruth was a classic case of love at first sight. She had stopped at the church to meet a friend who was involved in a committee meeting. More than a half-century later Norman romantically recalled the scene:

> Suddenly the doors at the rear of the sanctuary opened, and a girl stood framed in the golden light. I looked up and forgot everything. I stood transfixed. That was the girl. I had never seen her before, did not know her name. But I did know who she was; she was for me. From that minute, when she stood in that effulgent light, I fell in love with Ruth Stafford. She was waiting for one of the girls in my committee meeting, but actually it was I who was waiting for her. And I had been waiting for a long time.[7]

Ruth's reaction was not so immediate as Norman's. Indeed, she had subconsciously resisted the thought of marrying a minister. Her own memories of life in a parsonage had been happy ones, but the low financial remuneration was something she did not want to repeat in her own life. Norman, however, was persistent. He invited her to accompany him on speaking engagements, and her interest in him quickly intensified. To her mother she wrote:

> Now all this is just between you and me! He doesn't understand his sudden interest in the opposite sex, but while it lasts he is willing to take the consequences if I am! He is so frank that it is very amusing and refreshing. Thus I have a dinner engagement for Thursday. I am prepared to remain interested as long as he does. Now, I hope you smile over all this as I have smiled in writing it. I am not being kidded very much! And I'm thankful for the training my brothers gave me. The girls want to know when I shall begin calling him Norman![8]

Norman contacted a friend who was the superintendent of schools and was able to secure a teaching position in mathematics for Ruth so that she would not have to leave the Syracuse area after she graduated. Soon after that, they became engaged and two years later, in 1930, they had a June wedding in the University Church.[9]

Although they had known each other for most of three years before they married and they were both from Methodist ministers' families, their marriage was not without controversy. Norman's father was not only a Methodist minister, but also a district superintendent, whose salary was significantly higher than Ruth's father's. His mother was determined that her son do well, and that included marrying well. "She had great plans, great dreams for Norman," according to Ruth. "She had accepted the restrictions of life as a small-town minister's wife herself, but she believed her oldest boy had the seeds of greatness in him. She was not unconscious of the value of wealth and social position—and when she looked at me, she could see neither in my family background."[10]

Mrs. Peale's objections to Ruth were probably no greater than those she would have found in any young woman her son had chosen to marry. The fact is, Norman was what might be termed a "mama's boy." He had an overbearing mother, and Ruth had an extraordinary amount of patience to endure with grace her frequent interference. Mrs. Peale traveled to Syracuse to hear her son preach on his first Sunday there, and she returned again on Mother's Day. In many ways she lived vicariously through him.

Though she had strongly objected to his marrying Ruth, that factor did not stop her and Mr. Peale from joining them on their honeymoon; thus they all spent a week together in a remote, isolated cabin in the Adirondack Mountains. Whether Ruth truly "made no objection," as Norman's biographer suggests, is hard to take at face value, but at least in the end she did accept the arrangement and joined the three Peales for a week in the woods. A few years later, when Ruth and Norman took their first trip abroad, they were again accompanied by Mrs. Peale.[11]

The differences in family social standing and the mother-in-law problems were not the only difficulties Ruth faced as she entered marriage. She quickly discovered that Norman was much more indecisive than she. "I never had any problem making up my mind about almost anything," she wrote later, "but he had a hard time making decisions." Frequently when she thought he had made a decision after a long period of discussing the matter, she was jolted the next day to find that he was still as undecided as he had been before. "Then there were times when plans had been made and I was well along in carrying them out and suddenly Norman would tell me that something had come up to change it all. . . . This became a major adjustment for me, a fundamental clash in personal characteristics."[12]

One of Ruth's first enduring encounters with her husband's indecisiveness came soon after they were married. Two attractive pastoral calls came to him from churches on opposite sides of the country—one from the First Methodist Church of Los Angeles (the largest Methodist church in the country), the other from Marble Collegiate Church in New York (one of the oldest churches in the country). Ruth and Norman had been happy in their five years of ministry at the University Church in Syracuse until the new opportunities suddenly emerged. Then there was the prolonged ordeal of deciding which of the two to accept or whether to turn them both down. It would not have been an easy decision even for a decisive person, but the process was particularly painful for Norman, who was characterized by "indecision, a tendency to vacillate, a reluctance to make up his mind. . . . unable to move in any direction."[13]

The weeks went by as Norman "made up his mind and then unmade it quite a few times." It was a "nerve-wracking strain" for

Ruth and other family members as well as the churches in question. Finally Ruth decided the indecision could go on no longer. After lunch one day, she closed the door to the living room and gave an ultimatum: they simply could not go on vacillating between the choices. They would stay in that room as long as it took to come to a decision, and they would trust God to intervene and show them what was right.

The couple stayed in the room praying and talking and meditating and reading the Bible for hours. At last, "far into the evening," there was "a sudden relaxation of tension." Norman was convinced God wanted him to take the much smaller church in New York, and Ruth concurred.[14]

Norman's overcautious concern in decision making was equaled only by his demand for orderliness. "It doesn't bother me," Ruth confessed, "if the morning newspaper is still on the coffee table at night. But not Norman! His creativity simply stops if anything is out of order." For his writing and preaching, he needed to have his thoughts and ideas in "orderly sequence," so to oblige him, Ruth kept the "entire house in perfect order at all times. (I never knew which room he would look in next!)"[15] Because of her commitment to his ministry and her belief that he had boundless potential, Ruth perceived it to be her responsibility to cater to his quirks.

More troubling to Ruth than his indecisiveness and extreme orderliness was Norman's tendency to become despondent. Many people thought it impossible to believe that the prophet of positive thinking would suffer from dark periods of despair. Indeed, on one occasion a woman shared with Ruth the struggle she faced when her husband went into melancholy. Of course, she did not expect Ruth to be able to identify with the situation, but Ruth clarified that misconception: "When he gets depressed, he sees only the negative side of everything. Sometimes I think he writes about positive thinking because he understands so much about negative thinking!"[16]

How, then, could Norman be so effective in communicating the techniques of positive thinking? Regarding his dark moods, Ruth wrote, "I consider it part of my job as a wife to understand all this, to evaluate it unemotionally, and then do something about it. . . . I think the wife is the one who can set the emotional climate of the home. Basically, women are more stable emotionally than men. . . . Women are not so vulnerable to disappointment."[17] So behind the scenes, it was Ruth's job to keep her preacher-husband on a steady keel so that publicly he could reach millions in his preaching and writing.

Ruth has defended this role as the primary duty of a pastor's wife. In speaking of a pastor who was unhappy and had failed miserably in his profession after getting involved with another woman, she placed much of the blame on his wife. "Under such circumstances, her primary job was not to go around doing good deeds in the community. It was to sense her man's distress and seek a remedy for it, even if it meant changing her way of life completely. But she failed to do this, and one day her way of life blew up in her face."[18]

Despite this philosophy, Ruth herself was very active in "doing good deeds in the community." Initially, church work had not come easily for her. Although she was raised in a pastor's home, Ruth had very little interest in church matters and virtually no experience in heading committees or women's groups. But that quickly changed, and it was in this area that she became a great asset to her husband. Her desire to make up for his deficiencies in organizational duties thrust her into the forefront. She discovered that she was highly skilled in leading discussions and chairing meetings. She could analyze problems quickly and move toward a solution without becoming bogged down in the details.[19]

Ruth's abilities in organizational work proved valuable in various fund-raising projects and service ministries that she directed over her long tenure as a pastor's wife. She headed a quarter-million-dollar fund drive for a chapel at the Interchurch Center in New York and made similar efforts at Marble Collegiate Church. She likewise founded and directed the Foundation for Christian Living, for which her husband praised her highly: "By her faith, administrative ability, and executive skills as well as her dedication and love of people, she has built this great Christian service agency into the most outstanding institution of its kind in the history of Christianity in America." Another area of activity for Ruth was her editorial and administrative work with *Guideposts* magazine. Norman had taken the responsibility of that magazine's publication, and she served for decades as the magazine's executive vice-president.[20]

Despite her active involvement in church activities, Ruth viewed her domestic duties as her primary responsibility. Her superb organizational ability allowed her to accomplish much in addition to caring for the needs of her fastidious husband and their three children. Yet family life was amazingly casual and fun. Vacation times were frequent and relaxing, and family ties were close. Her most pressing commitment, however, was to provide the strength her husband needed to sustain his ministry.

The Peales's first years at Marble Collegiate Church were stressful ones. The pews in that grand old church were mainly empty, and many of those who did attend were older people in or nearing retirement. Norman vowed that his purpose was "not to fill seats but to fill souls with the Gospel of the Lord Jesus Christ," yet he could not help regretting the lack of immediate growth in numbers. Had he taken the church in California, he knew he would be packing the sanctuary for two services each Sunday, and he would be among his own people—the Methodists. In coming to New York, he had not only chosen a much smaller congregation, but also had moved into a new denomination—the Reformed Church in America.[21]

Further complicating their situation in New York was the state of the nation's economy. The stock market crash a few years earlier had taken its toll. "It was a bleak city and a bleak church. . . . Men were selling apples on street corners. Women were wearing out shoe leather looking for jobs that didn't exist. Heart attacks and nervous breakdowns were daily occurrences. Fear and anxiety were everywhere."[22] But Norman and Ruth had come to New York because they were convinced that with God's help they could turn a stagnant church around. And that is what they were determined to do.

Before that was accomplished, however, there were deep waters to pass through. After more than a year of "dealing with the dismal condition of the Marble Collegiate Church," they took a vacation to England. "I was restless and depressed regarding the church back in New York," Norman writes. "It seemed a hopeless situation. . . . In a gloomy manner I poured my woes into the ears of my happy and positive young wife. . . . Ruth proceeded to do a masterful job of therapy upon me." In his words, she was "firm and authoritative." She rebuked him:

> You are not only my husband. You are also my pastor, and in the latter department I'm frank to say I am becoming increasingly disappointed in you. I hear you from the pulpit talking about faith and trust in God's wondrous power. But now I hear in you no faith or trust at all. You just whine your defeat.

What jolted Norman the most in her scolding was her insistence that he needed to be "converted." "I have been converted," Norman retorted. "Well, it didn't take, so you had better get really converted," she snapped back.[23]

It is unusual for a "conversion" to take place in the midst of such a heated exchange, but according to Norman that is exactly what happened. "So in a stumbling sort of way, I confessed all my weaknesses, entreating the Lord to come to me, defeated as I was. . . . And the prayer was answered instantly. I began to feel warm all over from the crown of my head to my feet."[24]

This intensely emotional experience would not signal an end to Norman's dark moods, but it did help him to understand his weakness better. Soon after the publication of his best-selling book *The Power of Positive Thinking*, he plummeted to another low point. Although the book became more popular and far more widely circulated than the Peales had ever dreamed it would be, it initially received some harsh reviews from fellow churchmen. Conservative Evangelicals in many cases said it was without biblical foundation, and some liberals charged that it was an attempt to make a Christian defense of capitalistic materialism.[25]

Ruth desperately sought to shield Norman from the criticism that she knew would thrust him into despair, but to no avail. One article was particularly scurrilous, and when Norman read it he became so upset that he vowed to quit the Christian ministry. In fact, he wrote a letter of resignation to present to the church. Compounding Norman's despair over his critics was the serious illness of his father. It was his father's death, however, that brought Norman back to a sense of reality. At the funeral his stepmother told him that his father, before he died, had sensed Norman was facing a crisis, so he asked that a message be given his son: "The Peales never quit." Those words gave Norman the reassurance he needed, and he did not carry out the threat to resign.[26]

Ruth Peale has been unusually open about certain problems pastors' wives face that are rarely talked about. Although she has been her husband's strongest supporter, she treats him realistically in print—not giving him the super-saint image that so many wives of public men are prone to do. It is perhaps because she is so confident of his reputation that she can be so open about the marital problems they struggled with behind the walls of the parsonage. She has never pretended that they had a perfect marriage and, in fact, has been suspicious of other ministerial families who would claim they do.

> Countless times, talking with a married couple I've just met, I've heard them say to me, "Oh, yes, we've been married fifteen years (or twenty, or thirty) and we've never had a cross word between us." I always smile and nod happily, but what I'm really thinking is, "How dull! How boring! What a drag a marriage like that would be."

But while she contends that "disagreement between married partners can actually be constructive and useful," she readily concedes that "people say and do things in anger that can damage any relationship, sometimes permanently."[27]

The sparks sometimes flew in Ruth's relationship with Norman, as she candidly admitted to young wives who came to her for counseling. "I am always amused at their assumption," she wrote, "that being a minister's wife, I have never heard an angry or unkind word from my husband. . . . When we were first married . . . he could be very hard to live with. . . . When Norman was short-tempered or irritable, I had a tendency to flare up in return." Ruth felt it was primarily her responsibility to make peace. "The main lesson I learned from all this was that if I wanted the battle or the black mood to end quickly, I had to control myself. If I cut off the fuel by refusing to become angry or fight back, the whole thing blew over much more quickly."[28]

Ruth devoutly believed that it was primarily the wife's responsibility to make a marriage work—an outlook that would not appeal to contemporary feminists. But she made no effort to cater to feminists or feminist ideology. She strongly spoke against what she regarded as a perversion of male-female relationships. "To all militant feminists," she wrote, "I would just say this: Ladies, your real enemy in your search for happiness is not masculine prejudice, or masculine exploitation, or masculine anything. Your real enemy is the lack of femininity in you."[29]

In espousing femininity, Ruth was at the same time strong and successful in her own right, and she did more than anyone else to uphold an often weak husband who was listened to and read by millions, and who turned a lifeless empty church into a vibrant congregation that could not fit into the overflowing sanctuary. Indeed, "it became necessary to supply church members with tickets which gave them prior admission up to twenty minutes before the service began."[30] Ruth knew well the supreme significance of the role of the pastor's wife, and she played that role with dignity.

JILL BRISCOE

· 14 ·
Jill Briscoe
Shaping an Effective
Husband-Wife Team

The position and role of pastor's wife are nebulous. If there is anything to be learned from nearly five centuries of Protestant pastoral ministry, it is that. But whatever the particular function or the specific ministry the pastor's wife fills, she has invariably found the most fulfillment when she and her husband are involved in true partnership. In developing that partnership, it is necessary for the husband to recognize his wife's gifts and abilities. Too many pastors, perhaps due to their own insecurities, feel threatened by wives whose ministry in certain areas far surpasses their own.

Some writers have suggested that the pastor and his wife are unique for their *lack* of equality in ministry, and this factor sets them apart from other married people. Alice Taylor writes:

> Unlike most marriages there will be a unique factor to this team. *There is only one captain.* No matter how talented or capable the minister's wife, she must always remember that she is not No. 1. A very fine, but rather egotistical clergyman once said to me, about his new bride, "I told her that she would have to be content to be the tail of the kite!" This is putting it a little more bluntly than necessary, but he had the right idea.[1]

While the vast majority of pastors' wives would never aspire to become "captain" (if, indeed, most churches have *anyone* with a rank comparable to captain), the fact of the matter is that some pastors' wives can do pastoral work more effectively than their husbands can. Clayton Bell suddenly recognized this "pastoral" gift in his wife during a time of tragedy in their congregation when a woman received the news that most of her family members had been killed in a plane crash. "How grateful I am for a wife who is sensitive to the needs of others," he wrote. "Peggy's creative common sense and practical piety enabled her to do what was needed at the moment. Her gift had never been more apparent to me than in our *joint ministry* to Stephanie." Bell realized that his own ministry was enhanced when it was a true partnership. "I'm extremely grateful to the Lord for a wife who shares my ministry with me. Peggy's perceptions and sensitivity have been great assets in ministering. . . . Because the Lord has equipped her with gifts, complementary to mine, I rejoice that we can share much of the ministry to bereaved people."[2]

It is this kind of partnership that has the potential for far-reaching pastoral ministry—the type of ministry that characterizes the teamwork of Jill and Stuart Briscoe.

In a day and age when many *pastors' wives* are seeking to get out from under the restrictions of that appellation, Jill Briscoe stands as a striking example of one who has turned the role into a ministry profession in its own right. She has charted new frontiers in the specialization of women's ministries, and she has given the male pastoral role that her husband executes so well a feminine balance that has been demonstrated since 1970 in their large and expanding work at Elmbrook Church near Milwaukee, Wisconsin.

Jill was committed to Christian ministry before she met Stuart Briscoe. After college she became a preschool teacher in a poor district in Liverpool, England. Here she was confronted with deplorable conditions that she could not turn her back on. One abused boy in particular caught her attention.

> So one day I took his hand and told him I was going to walk him home. I found an unbelievable hovel of a house. I knew I would never be the same again if I simply left my small charge behind and went home to my beautiful, clean home; and yet at the same time I also knew I would never be the same again if I tried to do something about it. . . . "Where's Mother," I asked the little boy. "She caught on fire," he answered casually! "She's in 'ospital. She was smokin'

and drunk too much and a rag got on fire." "That's where you start, my girl," I said to myself, and off we went to meet mother. She told me the government was going to help get them a better place to live, but they were low on the list and it could be months before anything was done. Then I met Dad, an older brother, and an older sister.

Who could care about such people, I wondered? *Only* God could really love them. God was going to have to stretch my capacity and make love happen in my heart—and He did! He just needed permission.[3]

In addition to her teaching, Jill worked with the teens in her church in Liverpool. It was while she was involved in this work that she met Stuart Briscoe at a youth retreat. Stuart, a banker who spent his spare time traveling in youth work, had offered to come and talk to her youth group when he came to Liverpool. "Eighteen happy months later there was no doubt left in either of our minds. We belonged together."[4]

The ecstasy of falling in love and getting married, however, was quickly jarred by reality. Jill was a strong independent woman, and immediately there were questions as to what her role as a wife would be. "Were there to be some things a woman was not allowed to do after *the knot* was tied that she had freely done when it was not a *knot?* Somehow I had thought that marriage was *not to be a knot* at all, but a meshing together of two strands of string— making them one smooth, strong piece. But here we were on our honeymoon, already tied in *knobbled knots* of conflict!" Jill's frustrations could have been echoed by countless other women who had just been jolted into a traditional Christian marriage:

> Did marriage relegate me forever to the passenger seat, merely reading the map while he drove all the way? Would Stuart be not only the bread winner—but *the only winner?* How could we begin to complement each other instead of competing when both of us had such strong gifts and personalities? Was a Christian wife supposed to wrap up her spiritual gifts and return them to the Sender with one hand while unwrapping the wedding gifts with the other?[5]

Jill's questions were not immediately answered. After their first child was born, Stuart decided to leave his secular work and join the staff at the youth retreat where he and Jill had met. They would become "missionaries" and join the ranks of those in "full-time Christian service." Here Jill's frustrations surfaced again: "I began to wonder all over again about my role. Looking at the structure of the mission, I commented to Stuart that it didn't appear to be the accepted thing for a woman to be up front teaching and preaching." His response was what she did not want to hear. "Why don't you start practicing your gifts where they are needed most and where you've proved them before"—outside the mission.[6]

It was this challenge that prompted Jill to continue to use the gifts she had exercised with youth before she was married, though at first she became involved only reluctantly. During their first decade of marriage Jill was alone much of the time with their three children while Stuart traveled some nine months each year preaching and doing evangelistic work. She was upset by his frequent absence and suggested that he stay at home and do his evangelistic work with teens at the nearby Cat's Whisker coffee bar. His suggestion that she take up the challenge herself transformed her life. "It was a new beginning. . . . My spare time bulged with positive activity. . . . I sat down and made a note of my daily routine and blocked off my spare time, setting it aside for God. Young people were finding Christ, and follow-up Bible studies began in our home."[7]

Jill's success with youth convinced her that God had demonstrated to her where she could concentrate her gifts. It initially did not matter that the youth center was a mile away, while right next door and across her backyard were neighbors that had not been evangelized. She excused herself for avoiding them because they were "little old ladies." But she could not get them off her mind, knowing that God cared as much for their souls as he did for the young peoples' souls.

"Reluctantly I gave in," Jill writes. "Next day while wheeling our baby Peter in his pram and clutching the sticky hand of four-year-old David, I began my intrepid spy work . . . and at last plucked up courage to knock on a few doors and invite the ladies to my cottage to read the Bible." The neighbors all responded positively, but on the appointed day no one came. Jill's initial response was to let the idea die with a natural death, but she became more deeply convicted about her unwillingness to reach these women. She persisted, and eventually she had dozens of women studying the Bible, including the daughters and granddaughters of these "little old ladies."[8]

Jill did not allow her ministry with women to interfere with her ministry to youth. Her home became a hangout for young people with problems, and practical Bible studies became a routine. "Day after day, week after week the young people came, bringing their friends (and enemies) with them." Eventually the group became so large that the meeting place was changed to a nearby barn. The ministry expanded as the teens reached out to younger children, and "soon we had six clubs led by teens in different locations throughout the town." Eventually drama teams were developed for street evangelism.

Jill herself had shunned the bold witnessing she was encouraging the teens to become involved in, but in an effort to be a model to them she often had to lead the way. On one occasion at a rock concert, she writes, "I heard myself asking if I might speak to the thousand teen-agers gyrating to the unbelievably loud rock music." Initially taken aback, the manager listened to her and then agreed. "Week after week young people found Christ in that place, and today they are in the vanguard of the youth work."[9]

The success of her ministry did not prevent Jill from having bitterness about Stuart's long absences. "I learned to wave my husband off on a three-month tour with just the right evangelical smile," she wrote, but "I stopped reading the Bible, . . . and I stopped praying." She became depressed and was on the verge of demanding that Stuart stay home more. It was only after she counseled with an older missionary and searched her own motives that she was able to come to terms with her circumstances. "A miracle had happened in my heart. My situation was acceptable! I was at peace."[10]

This independence and contentment in ministry helped to prepare Jill for her position as a pastor's wife. Yet in many ways she was utterly unprepared for such a role. Nor did Stuart initially have any real concept of what the role of the pastor's wife should be. His background was among the Plymouth Brethren, where "the elders led the worship, and women kept quiet, wore hats, and never trousers." Jill had attended the chapels with Stuart, but had not found a role model: "No, there wasn't a pastor's wife in that group to model myself by, that was for sure. To begin with there wasn't even a pastor!"[11]

Unlike many pastors, Stuart, despite his background, had encouraged his wife to develop her own gifts and carve out her own ministries. He had seen his mother "late in life . . . do things she had never done before—things she thought women should not do. But out of necessity she did them and to her amazement found herself wonderfully gifted." This had an impact on Stuart— so much so that over the years he has done some deep soul-searching on the question of women and ministry.

> Frankly, as a pastor, a husband and a father, I have a dread of burying someone else's talents, particularly those bestowed on women.
>
> Accordingly, I have tried to scrutinize my views, the place of tradition, the thrust of theology and the force of my prejudices. Repeatedly, I have come back to this fact: If the Lord has given gifts, I had better be careful about denying freedom for their exercise.
>
> More than that, I need to ensure that the women in my life have every encouragement from me to be what He called and gifted them to be. A major part of my life must be spent as a man, caring for, nurturing, encouraging and developing gifted women, because they aren't the only ones who will give account for their stewardship.
>
> As a man in a male-oriented church, I may one day be asked about *their* gifts, too. I would like to be able to say I did considerably more than burying.
>
> A talent is a terrible thing to waste.[12]

Unlike so many husbands, Stuart did not feel threatened by Jill's independent spirit, and he was convinced that she had a ministry obligation to others far more than to him in catering to his needs. He learned to live with less than perfect housekeeping— sometimes kitchen cabinets that were stuffed with "wet tennis shoes, the dog's dishes, and the like." He was proud of her accomplishments with youth and women's groups and the eternal value these activities possessed.[13]

Jill did not always regard her role of pastor's wife with appreciation. She deals with this issue in *There's a Snake in My Garden*—a book that cleverly addresses the problems of Satan's temptations through references to "the snake." She tells of her early years in the ministry and her irritation at being set apart from the other women in her congregation.

> I noticed that at social gatherings I was introduced as "the pastor's wife." Each time it happened the snake snickered and pointed out that the other ladies present were not introduced as "the grocer's wife" or "the road-sweeper's wife" or "the garbage collector's spouse"!
>
> "You're stuck with it," he hissed happily. "Every time you're given your title, a preconceived notion flashes across their minds. All of them will have varied ideas of just 'how' you ought to 'perform,' and as each will differ according to their church and cultural backgrounds, you will have to be a freak to keep them all happy!"[14]

If Jill suspected that others had preconceived ideas about what a preacher's wife ought to be, so did she. "I had imagined a shadowy mouselike 'personage living in a parsonage'" with her "hair firmly screwed into a bun, her flat shoes facilitating the many errands of mercy she must run." The duties that accompanied her role were clearly mapped out: "succoring the dying, mending other people's cast-off clothes for the poor missionaries," and "pressing the parson's Sunday suits." Moreover, there were certain talents and abilities that were automatically assumed: she "*must* play the piano," she "must sit in the leadership chair at *every* women's gathering," and "she must teach Sunday school."[15]

For Jill, it was essential that she "once and for all bury the image of 'the pastor's wife'" and use the gifts and abilities God had given her in ministries that could most effectively reach out to other people. In doing so, however, she served as a role model for others. She became a pastor's wife par excellence by her very effort in seeking to avoid the images that had come to surround that role.

In discovering the gifts she had, Jill also discovered the gifts she did not possess. This troubled her, because it often made her feel less than adequate for the many tasks expected of a pastor's wife. She quickly learned, however, to differentiate between gifts and duties—that "there were certain 'duties' that went along with" the "privileged position" of pastor's wife "for which she might not be gifted."

I didn't feel altogether ignorant as to my gifts. From past experience I knew that I had been blessed in starting things, exploring situations, moving into new areas in evangelistic outreach. I knew I had a gift of teaching and speaking and a gift of creative ideas for children and teens. But I was *not* a gifted administrator or committee member; I was not a good listener; and I could produce little "small talk" in company. Seeing that the latter gifts seemed to be the most obvious ones that would be required for my pastoral duties, I had considerable trepidation in my heart.[16]

In many instances, when Jill found herself involved in ministries for which she was not gifted, she discovered that the end result was beneficial:

The best I could do with those things was to do them as heartily as I could and as badly as I did. This engendered a most interesting reaction. Some women who had been sitting vegetating in a pew, and who possessed those very abilities that I didn't, would watch my sad efforts and come to me most sympathetically, saying, "Oh, Jill, I think you'd better let us help"—and that was the way I began to get some of the jobs done that needed doing around the place![17]

As she discovered where her gifts could best be used in the various ministries of the church, Jill also discovered areas of involvement she should avoid. She learned quickly, as many pastors' wives do not, that she was not "called" to be her husband's defense attorney. Indeed, one of the most difficult problems that Jill has had to come to terms with over the years has been criticism of her husband. No pastor is without his critics, and frequently the pastor's wife suffers more than the pastor himself. The criticism that hurt the most came from those within the church, and that began as soon as the pastoral "honeymoon" was over. She felt an almost constant dread that some family or individual would become disgruntled and leave the church and her husband would be blamed. But having someone leave the church was in some instances not the worst outcome. Some people stayed and became a "thorn in the flesh" to her and Stuart.

Within a year of our arrival at the church we found ourselves in the middle of a major issue: a change in the church constitution! Sitting in a pretty highly charged, emotional church meeting, I realized how deeply people were feeling. There was much discussion over a doctrinal point that to me was a secondary issue, having nothing to do with salvation. I watched people literally "leaving the church" from that gathering, and I was completely floored by the whole thing. . . .

Now, one thing my husband didn't need at that moment of time was intervention. But up I got, managed two sentences, then burst into tears!

Here Jill was confronted with the very problems many pastors' wives face: "my overreaction to criticism of my husband. . . . It was a far harder thing for me to take than criticism of myself."[18]

Despite her deficiencies, Jill took her new role of pastor's wife very seriously and began developing programs and ideas in areas where she knew she had strengths. Her first efforts involved teens, where her past experience gave her confidence. Her next significant opportunity for ministry came when a woman outside her church asked her to lead a home Bible study. That tiny group grew and eventually merged with a Bible study group from the church—though Jill insisted it meet in a "neutral" place. Initially they met in a bank basement and then moved to a theater to accommodate the larger crowds that in two years grew to four hundred women who faithfully attended each week.[19]

Jill's next venture was to plan a one-day women's retreat. With the help of two other women who led Bible studies in the church, she arranged to secure the facilities of a nearby Catholic school. Some nine hundred women attended. The next retreat—this time two days—was scheduled for the following January, and the attendance grew to more than two thousand women. For Jill, this was just the beginning of a newfound niche in women's ministries. "Doors of opportunity were opening up for me—speaking engagements that would take me all over the country. Up until now Stuart had been the traveler and I had stayed at home."[20]

This was clearly a new dimension to Jill's ministry, and it was not achieved without struggles and problems. Catherine Marshall had also traveled the country speaking, but only after Peter died. Jill and Stuart suddenly found themselves struggling with the complications of a two-career marriage. Jill was excited about her out-of-town opportunities, but there was always stress in leaving the family behind: "the vision of Judy falling off her bike, or David and Peter having fights no one refereed, or Stuart not being able to find either of his preaching suits because I'd forgotten to pick them up from the cleaners!" She soon discovered, however, that the family was able to manage without her constant presence—a discovery aided by a supportive husband.[21]

An issue that Jill confronted almost immediately, once she began speaking widely, was the proper role of women in ministry. Although her husband had been supportive of her varied ministries, she was forced to face the questions herself. Was it proper (and biblical) for a woman to be traveling as a Bible teacher? Even though her audiences were made up mainly of women, the issue was a controversial one. "Now this was not a new problem to me," she writes. "Almost as soon as I became a Christian I heard totally opposing views about the matter. One group I met with refused to let ladies even pray aloud in a mixed group, and yet this same church allowed their missionary women to preach, teach, and pray out in 'darkest Africa.' "[22]

There were other inconsistencies as well: "ladies were forbidden to speak to a 'group' of men but were expected to witness on a one-to-one basis! What difference did plurality make, I wondered." In her study of the issue, Jill concluded that "the big scriptural prohibition appeared to be the principle of usurping the authority of the man," and she concluded that she was not counteracting that principle in her ministry.[23]

Jill developed her own style of speaking—or some might say lack of style. She was tempted at times to share her own personal experiences or tell fascinating stories about others to generate more excitement in her presentations. But while she recognized the value of this for other speakers, she herself was not comfortable with that method: "I was to preach the Word, not my experience!"[24]

One of Jill's strengths in ministry has been her ability to turn what might have been a disaster into a success and to go a step beyond that to see in negative situations possibilities for further ministry. One such incident involved a Sunday night women's meeting she had agreed to take without inquiring about details. Arriving late (after being stuck in a snowdrift) at the address she had scribbled on a piece of paper, she discovered she was at a bowling alley. She was ushered into a back room only to find she was in a social club, and the group was engaged in wine tasting. "After quite a while, a little man got up and said, 'Now then, I see our speaker has arrived. I'm afraid I don't know anything about her.' He stopped and suddenly appeared to remember something. 'Oh, yes, I do,' he countered. 'I think she's got a comedy act!'" On her way to the podium, the man handed her a wine bottle that still had some wine in it.[25]

How could she speak in a situation like that and make her words meaningful? Jill used the circumstances to make her point of contact. From the wine-tasting episode she had just observed, she focused their attention of the story of changing water into wine at the wedding of Cana, and from that lead-in began dealing with the subject of Christian marriage. She received a mixed reaction, but the important lesson she learned was that here in this secular setting she was finding people hungering to be fed the Word of God.

That night proved to be a turning point in Jill's ministry. She began an investigation of social clubs in the Milwaukee area, and she and her committee sent letters to each one, offering holiday programs with a variety of alternatives—speaking, readings, drama, and music. With that bowling alley beginning, Jill opened a new avenue of community outreach.[26]

Jill's team ministry with her husband at the Elmbrook Church and in the neighborhood has continued to grow. By the late 1970s, Elmbrook Church had one of the most far-reaching women's ministries programs in the country. "Morning Break," held each Thursday, serves as a model for reaching "every" woman in the community. After the opening coffee break, Jill teaches the Bible lesson, which is followed by small groups led by women who are prepared to deal with individuals with specialized needs such as weight problems, alcohol and drug abuse, or marital breakdown. For women who are employed, there are "Brown Bag Bible Studies." There are also programs for young mothers and retired women. These activities along with women's retreats, a videotape library, and television programing were largely under Jill's supervision (in her unpaid lay capacity) until the spring of 1987, when the church, with Jill's encouragement, hired her assistant as Pastor of Women's Ministries.

Through her eighteen books, her frequent speaking engagements, and her active involvement in Elmbrook Church and community ministries, Jill has demonstrated what a pastor's wife can accomplish when there is true partnership in ministry. In many ways she is the exception to the rule, but she would not want to view herself as such. Training other pastoral couples is part of the ministry of the Briscoes at Elmbrook, and in her ministry to women and other pastors' wives, Jill makes it a priority to share her insights and specific ideas and programs so that others may more effectively serve in their own spheres of ministry.

• Conclusion •

It goes without saying that only a minute fraction of the vast multitude of pastor's wives who have lived and died during the past five centuries are mentioned in this volume. Countless women have served faithfully and have long been forgotten by all but God, who will surely reward them as "good and faithful servants."

One such dear woman was Charlotte Selina Bompass, who served with her husband, an Anglican bishop, in Northwest Canada in the late nineteenth century. "Frail in body though she was, her endurance and perseverance were remarkable. On the verge of starvation, she sometimes had to depend for food from day to day, on the rabbit snare and the daily dole of the meagre fish net." Charlotte was often left alone as her husband traveled about his 750,000-square-mile diocese, but she kept busy in her teaching ministry, her men's club work, and her women's work. In fact, she started the first Yukon branch of the Woman's Auxiliary. On one occasion, "owing to low water and early freeze-up," Charlotte was stranded and had to spend the winter separated from her husband. She was able to stay with a minister's family, but because they "only had two rooms, and four boys as well, a lean-to had to be erected for Mrs. Bompass in the schoolhouse which she found quite chilly, to say the least. However, she busied herself and taught school daily."[1]

Another woman whose past ministry has been all but lost to the present generation is Jessie Bartlett Hess. Jessie married a Methodist-turned-Presbyterian preacher in 1909, and forty-five years later was selected in second place for New York State's "Mother of the Year" award. During the interim she had a full and active ministry as a pastor's wife. She and her husband's ministry in the early years involved planting a dozen churches "in the flea-bitten faraway places in the west." During those years she served as a full partner in pastoral ministry, but she was not recognized as such. During times when her husband was ill or unable to preach, she did have the necessary credentials to take his place, having studied for the ministry at Moody Bible Institute and at Winona Lake, Indiana. Thus in 1929, in addition to her duties as a pastor's wife, she became a pastor in her own right—through the Congregational Church, because her own Presbyterian denomination did not permit the ordination of women. Jessie's first charge was a tiny Congregational church in Tonganoxie, Kansas. In the years that followed, and as her husband's health deteriorated, she continued in pastoral ministry; after his death she taught several large women's Bible classes in the New York metropolitan area.[2]

There have been countless other pastors' wives who have served sacrificially in their spheres of ministry—from the remote Anglican diocese to the inner-city Pentecostal storefront, from the suburban Baptist super-church to the rural Congregational chapel. Although they were sometimes accorded very little honor, they were, nevertheless, "first ladies"; and in most instances the parish was much richer because of their presence.

Most of these women were full partners in the pastoral ministry. They were heavily involved in the daily duties of the pastorate, and problems in the church frequently affected them as much or more than they did their husbands. Although these women were unpaid and had no official recognition, their calling was a consuming, full-time ministry. Indeed, in many ways they were no less involved in sacrificial ministry than were their single sisters who would span the globe in foreign missionary service. But unlike them, they would not be remembered in their own right—as pastors' wives. Mary Slessor, Lottie Moon, Amy Carmichael, and Gladys Aylward have been properly honored in their own right, but pastors' wives have been lost in obscurity or remembered only because of their husbands' fame or, like Susanna Wesley, their sons' fame. Yet in many instances they served with distinction no less than their husbands, and history has done them a disservice by forgetting their names and diminishing the importance of their ministries.

May this book be a model for other books not yet written—books telling the stories of pastors' wives who have served with distinction but have been lost in history. We will be much richer in our own spiritual pilgrimages if the stories of women like Charlotte Bompass and Jessie Bartlett Hess are preserved for our own edification and for posterity.

• Notes •

Introduction

[1] Lora Lee Parrott, *How to Be a Preacher's Wife and Like It* (Grand Rapids: Zondervan, 1956), 44–45.

[2] Jill Briscoe, *There's a Snake in My Garden* (Grand Rapids: Zondervan, 1975), 89.

[3] Karen Burton Mains, *Open Heart, Open Home* (Elgin, Ill.: David C. Cook, 1976), 21.

[4] Marilyn Brown Oden, *The Minister's Wife: Person or Position?* (Nashville: Abingdon, 1966), 27.

[5] Alice Taylor, *How to Be a Minister's Wife and Love It* (Grand Rapids: Zondervan, 1968), 16.

[6] Leonard I. Sweet, *The Minister's Wife: Her Role in Nineteenth-Century American Evangelicalism* (Philadelphia: Temple University Press, 1983), 3, 91.

[7] Denise Turner, *Home Sweet Fishbowl: Confessions of a Minister's Wife* (Waco, Tex.: Word, 1982), 42.

[8] Ellen Goodman, "What's With the Nancy-bashing?" *Grand Rapids Press* (19 March 1987): E4.

Part I. Ministry Goals

[1] Denise Turner, *Home Sweet Fishbowl: Confessions of a Minister's Wife* (Waco, Tex.: Word, 1982), 57.

[2] Ibid., 21.

Chapter 1. Katie Luther

[1] Denise Turner, *Home Sweet Fishbowl: Confessions of a Minister's Wife* (Waco, Tex.: Word, 1982), 80.

[2] Charlotte Ross, *Who Is the Minister's Wife?: A Search for Personal Fulfillment* (Philadelphia: Westminster, 1980), 78, 81.

[3] Frances Nordland, *The Unprivate Life of a Pastor's Wife* (Chicago: Moody, 1972), 154.

[4] Quoted in Richard Friedenthal, *Luther: His Life and Times*, trans. John Nowell (New York: Harcourt Brace Jovanovich, 1970), 438.

[5] E. G. Schwiebert, *Luther and His Times* (St. Louis: Concordia, 1950), 584.

[6] Friedenthal, *Luther: His Life and Times*, 437.

[7] Roland H. Bainton, *Here I Stand: A Life of Martin Luther* (New York: Mentor Books, 1950), 223.

[8] Roland H. Bainton, *Women of the Reformation in Germany and Italy* (Minneapolis: Augsburg, 1971), 24.

[9] Schwiebert, *Luther and His Times*, 586–87.

[10] Ibid., 587.

[11] Ibid.

[12] Ibid., 588.

[13] Ibid., 589.

[14] Theodore J. Kleinhans, *Martin Luther: Saint and Sinner* (London: Marshall, Morgan and Scott, 1959), 105.

[15] Bainton, *Women of the Reformation*, 27.

[16] Schwiebert, *Luther and His Times*, 590.

[17] Philip Schaff, *History of the Christian Church*, 8 vols. (Grand Rapids: Wm. B. Eerdmans, 1979), 8:417.

[18] Schwiebert, *Luther and His Times*, 591.

[19] Bainton, *Women of the Reformation*, 26, 29.

[20] Ibid., 30.

[21] Schwiebert, *Luther and His Times*, 595.

[22] Ibid., 597.

[23] Friedenthal, *Luther: His Life and Times*, 439–40.

[24] Leonard I. Sweet, *The Minister's Wife: Her Role in Nineteenth-Century American Evangelicalism* (Philadelphia: Temple University Press, 1983), 14.

[25] Schwiebert, *Luther and His Times*, 599–600.

[26] Ibid., 601.

Chapter 2. Katherine Zell

[1] Leonard I. Sweet, *The Minister's Wife: Her Role in Nineteenth-Century American Evangelicalism* (Philadelphia: Temple University Press, 1983), 150–51.

[2] Karen Burton Mains, *Open Heart, Open Home* (Elgin, Ill.: David C. Cook, 1976), 21–22.

[3] Quoted in Julia O'Faolain and Lauro Martines, eds., *Not in God's Image* (New York: Harper and Row, 1973), 204.

[4] Mariam V. Chrisman, "Women of the Reformation in Strassburg, 1490–1530," *Archive for Reformation History* 63 (1972): 152–53.

[5] Roland H. Bainton, *Women of the Reformation in Germany and Italy* (Minneapolis: Augsburg, 1971), 61.

[6] Ibid.

[7] Ibid., 63.

[8] Donald K. McKim, "Disturber of the Peace: A Profile of Katherine Zell, Unknown Reformer," *Eternity* (June 1984): 30.

[9] Bainton, *Women of the Reformation*, 73.

[10] Philip Schaff, *History of the Christian Church*, 8 vols. (Grand Rapids: Wm. B. Eerdmans, 1979), 7:633.

[11] Bainton, *Women of the Reformation*, 64–65.

[12] Chrisman, "Women of the Reformation," 156.

[13] Bainton, *Women of the Reformation,* 66–67.

[14] Ibid., 67.

[15] Ibid.

[16] Ibid., 68.

[17] McKim, "Disturber of the Peace," 30.

[18] Bainton, *Women of the Reformation,* 72.

[19] Ibid., 69.

[20] Chrisman, "Women of the Reformation," 157–58.

Chapter 3. Idelette Calvin

[1] Gail MacDonald, *High Call, High Privilege* (Wheaton, Ill.: Tyndale House, 1981), 92.

[2] Betty J. Coble, *The Private Life of a Minister's Wife* (Nashville: Broadman, 1981), 104.

[3] Georgia Harkness, *John Calvin: The Man and His Ethics* (Nashville: Abingdon, 1958), 16.

[4] Thea B. Van Halsema, *This Was John Calvin* (Grand Rapids: Baker, 1981), 113.

[5] William J. Peterson, "Idelette: John Calvin's Search for the Right Wife," *Christian History* 5, no. 4 (1986): 13.

[6] Ibid.

[7] Van Halsema, *This Was John Calvin,* 115.

[8] Petersen, "Idelette," 13.

[9] Van Halsema, *This Was John Calvin,* 115–17.

[10] Ibid., 97.

[11] Ibid., 98–99, 127–28, 133.

[12] Petersen, "Idelette," 14; Albert Hyma, *Life of John Calvin* (Grand Rapids: Wm. B. Eerdmans, 1943), 84–85.

[13] Hyma, *Life of John Calvin,* 85.

[14] Van Halsema, *This Was John Calvin,* 141.

[15] Williston Walker, *John Calvin: The Organizer of Reformed Protestantism, 1509–1564* (New York: Schocken, 1969), 263.

[16] T. H. L. Parker, *John Calvin: A Biography* (Philadelphia: Westminster, 1975), 97–100.

[17] Petersen, "Idelette," 14; Harkness, *John Calvin: The Man and His Ethics,* 136.

[18] Petersen, "Idelette," 14.

[19] Van Halsema, *This Was John Calvin,* 147.

[20] Ibid., 148.

[21] Petersen, "Idelette," 15.

[22] Parker, *John Calvin: A Biography,* 102.

[23] Petersen, "Idelette," 15.

[24] Ibid.

[25] Walker, *John Calvin: The Organizer of Reformed Protestantism, 1509–1564,* 236.

[26] Petersen, "Idelette," 15.

[27] Parker, *John Calvin: A Biography,* 102.

Part II. Ministry Problems

¹Dorothy Harrison Pentecost, *The Pastor's Wife and the Church* (Chicago: Moody Press, 1964), 45.

²Ibid., 52.

Chapter 4. Susanna Wesley

¹David Mace and Vera Mace, *What's Happening to Clergy Marriages?* (Nashville: Abingdon, 1980), 21.

²Denise Turner, *Home Sweet Fishbowl: Confessions of a Minister's Wife* (Waco, Tex.: Word, 1982), 102–3.

³Ibid., 107.

⁴Rebecca L. Harmon, *Susanna: Mother of the Wesleys* (Nashville: Abingdon, 1968), 20.

⁵Charles Wallace, Jr., "Susanna Wesley's Spirituality: The Freedom of a Christian Woman," *Methodist History* 22 (April 1984): 163.

⁶Harmon, *Susanna: Mother of the Wesleys,* 47–49.

⁷Ibid., 47.

⁸Robert G. Tuttle, Jr., *John Wesley: His Life and Theology* (Grand Rapids: Zondervan, 1978), 41.

⁹Ibid., 42.

¹⁰Wallace, "Susanna Wesley's Spirituality," 158.

¹¹Ibid., 164.

¹²Harmon, *Susanna: Mother of the Wesleys,* 89.

¹³John Wesley, *The Works of John Wesley,* 13 vols. (Grand Rapids: Zondervan, 1958), 1:385.

¹⁴Ibid., 386.

¹⁵Ibid.

¹⁶Ibid.

¹⁷Ibid.

¹⁸Wallace, "Susanna Wesley's Spirituality," 161.

¹⁹Ibid., 162.

²⁰Harmon, *Susanna: Mother of the Wesleys,* 105–6.

²¹Ibid., 102–137.

Chapter 5. Mary Fletcher

¹Charlotte Ross, *Who Is the Minister's Wife: A Search for Personal Fulfillment* (Philadelphia: Westminster Press, 1980), 117.

²Earl Kent Brown, *Women of Mr. Wesley's Methodism* (New York: Edwin Mellen, 1983), 50.

³John Wesley to Mary Fletcher, 13 January 1786, in John Wesley, *The Works of John Wesley,* 13 vols. (Grand Rapids: Zondervan, 1959), 12:408.

⁴Henry Moore, *The Life of Mrs. Mary Fletcher* (New York: Hunt and Eaton, 1817), 32.

⁵Brown, *Women of Mr. Wesley's Methodism,* 134–38; Moore, *The Life of Mrs. Mary Fletcher,* 45.

⁶Brown, *Women of Mr. Wesley's Methodism,* 139–40.

⁷Jabez Burns, *Life of Mrs. Fletcher* (London: Joseph Smith, 1853), 37.

⁸Brown, *Women of Mr. Wesley's Methodism,* 142.

⁹Ibid., 142–44.

¹⁰Joseph Benson, *The Life of the Rev. John W. de la Fléchère* (New York: Carlton and Phillips, 1853), 274.

[11] Ibid., 276.

[12] Bessie Olson, *John Fletcher, the Great Saint* (Des Moines: Boone Publishing, 1944), 16.

[13] Brown, *Women of Mr. Wesley's Methodism*, 144.

[14] Moore, *The Life of Mrs. Mary Fletcher*, 148.

[15] Olson, *John Fletcher, the Great Saint*, 33.

[16] Brown, *Women of Mr. Wesley's Methodism*, 145.

[17] Ibid., 20, 23–24.

[18] Ibid., 29.

[19] Ibid., 27–28.

[20] Benson, *The Life of the Rev. John W. de la Fléchère*, 289–92; Brown, *Women of Mr. Wesley's Methodism*, 77.

[21] Brown, *Women of Mr. Wesley's Methodism*, 145–46.

[22] Ibid., 146–47.

[23] Moore, *The Life of Mrs. Mary Fletcher*, 172.

[24] Brown, *Women of Mr. Wesley's Methodism*, 148.

[25] Leonard I. Sweet, *The Minister's Wife: Her Role in Nineteenth-Century American Evangelicalism* (Philadelphia: Temple University Press, 1983), 84.

[26] Brown, *Women of Mr. Wesley's Methodism*, 151.

[27] Zachariah Taft, *Biographical Sketches of the Lives and Public Ministry of Various Holy Women*, 2 vols. (London: Dershaw, 1825; Leeds: Cullingworth, 1828), 2:27.

[28] Burns, *Life of Mrs. Fletcher*, 127–28.

[29] Moore, *The Life of Mrs. Mary Fletcher*, 247–48.

[30] Brown, *Women of Mr. Wesley's Methodism*, 154.

Chapter 6. Sarah Edwards

[1] Lora Lee Parrott, *How to Be a Preacher's Wife and Like It* (Grand Rapids: Zondervan, 1956), 26.

[2] Ibid., 26–27.

[3] Denise Turner, *Home Sweet Fishbowl: Confessions of a Minister's Wife* (Waco, Tex.: Word, 1982), 148.

[4] Turner, *Home Sweet Fishbowl*, 44–45.

[5] Jonathan Edwards, "Sarah Pierrpont," in *Jonathan Edwards, Representative Selections*, ed. Clarence H. Faust and Thomas H. Johnson, rev. ed. (New York: Hill and Wang, 1962), 56.

[6] Elizabeth D. Dodds, *Marriage to a Difficult Man: The "Uncommon Union" of Jonathan and Sarah Edwards* (Philadelphia: Westminster, 1971), 11–12.

[7] Amanda Porterfield, *Feminine Spirituality in America: From Sarah Edwards to Martha Graham* (Philadelphia: Temple University Press, 1980), 49.

[8] Dodds, *Marriage to a Difficult Man*, 29.

[9] S. E. Dwight, *The Life of President Edwards* (New York: G. and C. and H. Carvill, 1830), 128–29.

[10] Ibid., 128, 130–31.

[11] Dodds, *Marriage to a Difficult Man*, 40.

[12] Ibid., 88–91.

[13] Ibid., 83, 90.

[14] Leonard I. Sweet, *The Minister's Wife: Her Role in Nineteenth-Century American Evangelicalism* (Philadelphia: Temple University Press, 1983), 95.

[15] Dwight, *The Life of President Edwards*, 176.

[16] Ola Elizabeth Winslow, *Jonathan Edwards, 1703–1758: A Biography* (New York: Macmillan, 1940), 204.

[17] Dodds, *Marriage to a Difficult Man*, 29–30.

[18] Ibid., 98.

[19] Ibid., 140–41.

[20] Ibid., 143.

[21] Winslow, *Jonathan Edwards, 1703–1758*, 241–60.

[22] Dodds, *Marriage to a Difficult Man*, 159.

Chapter 7. Eunice Beecher

[1] Naomi Taylor Wright with Dick Bohrer, "Let's Let Women Counsel Women," *Moody Monthly* (November 1980): 41–42.

[2] Frances Nordland, *The Unprivate Life of a Pastor's Wife* (Chicago: Moody Press, 1972), 109–110.

[3] William C. Beecher and Rev. Samuel Scoville, assisted by Mrs. Henry Ward Beecher, *A Biography of Henry Ward Beecher* (New York: Charles L. Webster, 1888), 121–23.

[4] Beecher and Scoville, *A Biography of Henry Ward Beecher*, 124–25.

[5] Ibid., 125–27.

[6] Ibid., 169.

[7] Paxton Hibben, *Henry Ward Beecher: An American Portrait* (New York: George H. Doran, 1927), 57–58, 66.

[8] Beecher and Scoville, *A Biography of Henry Ward Beecher*, 169–70.

[9] Ibid., 172–76.

[10] Hibben, *Henry Ward Beecher*, 67–68.

[11] Ibid., 79, 98.

[12] Ibid., 108.

[13] Ibid., 120–21.

[14] Ibid., 144.

[15] Altina L. Waller, *Reverend Beecher and Mrs. Tilton: Sex and Class in Victorian America* (Amherst: University of Massachusetts Press, 1982), 34.

[16] Ibid., 31.

[17] Hibben, *Henry Ward Beecher*, 149, 176.

[18] Clifford E. Clark, Jr., *Henry Ward Beecher: Spokesman for Middle-Class America* (Urbana: University of Illinois, 1978), 172.

[19] Quoted in Waller, *Reverend Beecher and Mrs. Tilton*, 33.

[20] Hibben, *Henry Ward Beecher*, 176, 196.

[21] Ibid., 101, 244.

[22] Hibben, *Henry Ward Beecher*, 182–84, 187, 204; Beecher and Scoville, *A Biography of Henry Ward Beecher*, 502.

[23] Hibben, *Henry Ward Beecher*, 252, 229.

[24] Hibben, *Henry Ward Beecher*, 232, 238, 244–45; Beecher and Scoville, *A Biography of Henry Ward Beecher*, 508–9.

[25] Hibben, *Henry Ward Beecher*, 266–72; Beecher and Scoville, *A Biography of Henry Ward Beecher*, 530.

[26] Hibben, *Henry Ward Beecher*, 273–79, 292.

[27] Clark, *Henry Ward Beecher*, 223.

[28] Ibid., 244.

[29] Eunice Beecher, "Mr. and Mrs. Beecher's Plans," *Ladies' Home Journal* 9 (February 1892): 12.

Chapter 8. Margaret Simpson

[1] Denise Turner, *Home Sweet Fishbowl: Confessions of a Minister's Wife* (Waco, Tex.: Word, 1982), 121.

[2] A. W. Tozer, *Wingspread: A. B. Simpson, a Study in Spiritual Altitude* (Harrisburg: Christian Publications, 1943), 87.

[3] Robert L. Niklaus, John S. Sawin, and Samuel J. Stoesz, *All for Jesus: God at Work in the Christian and Missionary Alliance Over One Hundred Years* (Camp Hill, Pa.: Christian Publications, 1986), 26.

[4] A. E. Thompson, *The Life of A. B. Simpson* (New York: The Christian Alliance Publishing Co., 1920), 15.

[5] Niklaus, Sawin, and Stoesz, *All for Jesus,* 28.

[6] Gerald E. McGraw, *The Doctrine of Sanctification in the Published Writings of Albert Benjamin Simpson* (Ph.D. diss., New York University, 1986), 66.

[7] Thompson, *The Life of A. B. Simpson,* 51–53.

[8] Ibid., 120.

[9] Ibid., 121.

[10] Ibid., 57–62.

[11] McGraw, *The Doctrine of Sanctification,* 71.

[12] Niklaus, Sawin, and Stoesz, *All for Jesus,* 33–34.

[13] Ibid., 39–40.

[14] Ibid., 41–42.

[15] Ibid., 44.

[16] Tozer, *Wingspread,* 86–87.

[17] Niklaus, Sawin, and Stoesz, *All for Jesus,* 45.

[18] McGraw, *The Doctrine of Sanctification,* 79.

[19] Thompson, *The Life of A. B. Simpson,* 95–96; Niklaus, Sawin, and Stoesz, *All for Jesus,* 54.

[20] Thompson, *The Life of A. B. Simpson,* 190.

[21] Niklaus, Sawin, and Stoesz, *All for Jesus,* 57.

[22] Ibid., 57.

[23] Ibid., 34.

[24] Thompson, *The Life of A. B. Simpson,* 47–48.

[25] Niklaus, Sawin, and Stoesz, *All for Jesus,* 28.

[26] Ibid., 56, 60–61, 266, 273.

[27] McGraw, *The Doctrine of Sanctification,* 71–72.

[28] Tozer, *Wingspread,* 72, 141.

Part III. Ministry Challenges

[1] M. Scott Peck, *The Road Less Traveled: A New Psychology of Love, Traditional Values and Spiritual Growth* (New York: Simon and Schuster, 1978), 16.

[2] Betty J. Coble, *The Private Life of the Minister's Wife* (Nashville: Broadman, 1981), 127.

Chapter 9. Susannah Spurgeon

[1] "The Week of the Dragon," *Time* (16 March 1987): 24.

[2] "First Ladies Always Have Been Protective," *Grand Rapids Press* (9 March 1987): C.

[3] Marilyn Brown Oden, *The Minister's Wife: Person or Position?* (Nashville: Abingdon, 1966), 52.

[4] Arnold Dallimore, *Spurgeon* (Chicago: Moody Press, 1984), 55–59.

⁵ Patricia S. Kruppa, *Charles Haddon Spurgeon: A Preacher's Progress* (New York: Garland, 1982), 75–76, 106.

⁶ Dallimore, *Spurgeon*, 58.

⁷ Iain Murray, ed., *The Early Years* (London: Banner of Truth, 1962), 289.

⁸ Susannah Spurgeon and J. W. Harrald, comp., *C. H. Spurgeon's Autobiography*, 4 vols. (London: Passmore and Alabaster, 1897), 2:298.

⁹ C. H. Spurgeon, *The Early Years, 1834–1859*, vol. 1 of *Autobiography* (London: Banner of Truth Trust, 1962), 423.

¹⁰ Dallimore, *Spurgeon*, 71.

¹¹ Kruppa, *Charles Haddon Spurgeon*, 108.

¹² Dallimore, *Spurgeon*, 139.

¹³ Ibid., 65.

¹⁴ Ibid., 66.

¹⁵ Richard Ellsworth Day, *The Shadow of the Broad Brim: The Life Story of Charles Haddon Spurgeon, Heir of the Puritans* (Valley Forge: Judson Press, 1934), 136–37.

¹⁶ Kruppa, *Charles Haddon Spurgeon*, 187–88.

¹⁷ Russell H. Conwell, *Life of Charles Haddon Spurgeon* (N.p.: Edgewood, 1892), 251–52; George C. Needham, *The Life and Labors of Charles H. Spurgeon* (Boston: D. L. Guernsey, 1884), 530.

¹⁸ Conwell, *Life of Charles Haddon Spurgeon*, 251–52.

¹⁹ Spurgeon, *The Early Years*, 462–63, 144.

²⁰ Ibid., 364–65.

²¹ Needham, *Life and Labors*, 534–35.

²² Day, *Shadow of the Broad Brim*, 148–49.

²³ Ibid., 149.

²⁴ Dallimore, *Spurgeon*, 179–80.

²⁵ J. D. Fulton, *Spurgeon, Our Ally* (Chicago: H. J. Smith, 1892), 345.

²⁶ Dallimore, *Spurgeon*, 168.

²⁷ Kruppa, *Charles Haddon Spurgeon*, 110.

²⁸ Ibid.

²⁹ Spurgeon, *The Early Years*, 326–27.

Chapter 10. Emma Moody

¹ Frances Nordland, *The Unprivate Life of a Pastor's Wife* (Chicago: Moody Press, 1972), 107–8.

² Betty J. Coble, *The Private Life of the Minister's Wife* (Nashville, Broadman, 1981), 53.

³ J. C. Pollock, *Moody: A Biographical Portrait of the Pacesetter in Modern Mass Evangelism* (New York: Macmillan, 1963), 23–24.

⁴ Ibid., 28.

⁵ Emma Moody Powell, *Heavenly Destiny: The Life Story of Mrs. D. L. Moody* (Chicago: Moody Press, 1943), 37.

⁶ Richard K. Curtis, *They Called Him Mister Moody* (Grand Rapids: Wm. B. Eerdmans, 1962), 86.

⁷ Pollock, *Moody: A Biographical Portrait*, 28.

⁸ Ibid., 48.

⁹ J. Wilbur Chapman, *The Life and Work of Dwight L. Moody* (New York: Noble, 1900), 119.

¹⁰ W. H. Daniels, *Moody: His Words, Works, and Workers* (New York: Nelson and Phillips, 1977), 233.

[11] Pollock, *Moody: A Biographical Portrait*, 55.
[12] Edith Deen, *Great Women of the Christian Faith* (New York: Harper and Row, 1959), 385.
[13] James F. Findlay, Jr., *Dwight L. Moody: American Evangelist, 1837–1899* (Chicago: University of Chicago Press, 1969), 333–34.
[14] Ibid., 375.
[15] Ibid., 382–83.
[16] Ibid., 382n.
[17] Deen, *Great Women of the Christian Faith*, 385.
[18] C. H. Fowler, *D. L. Moody and His Work* (N.p.: n.p., 1875), 197–200.
[19] Pollock, *Moody: A Biographical Portrait*, 87–88.
[20] Ibid., 89.
[21] Ibid.
[22] Curtis, *They Called Him Mr. Moody*, 129, 142, 165–71.
[23] Pollock, *Moody: A Biographical Portrait*, 141.
[24] Powell, *Heavenly Destiny*, 146.
[25] Janette Hassey, *No Time for Silence: Evangelical Women in Public Ministry Around the Turn of the Century* (Grand Rapids: Zondervan, 1986), 33–35.
[26] Powell, *Heavenly Destiny*, 269.
[27] Findlay, *Dwight L. Moody*, 97.
[28] Deen, *Great Women of the Christian Faith*, 385.
[29] Ibid.

Chapter 11. Daisy Smith

[1] Donna Sinclair, *The Pastor's Wife Today* (Nashville: Abingdon, 1981), 27, 29.
[2] Leonard I. Sweet, *The Minister's Wife: Her Role in Nineteenth-Century American Evangelicalism* (Philadelphia: Temple University Press, 1983), 17.
[3] Hope Evangeline, *Daisy* (Grand Rapids: Baker, 1978), 33–34.
[4] Ibid., 45–46.
[5] Ibid., 46–49.
[6] Ibid., 53.
[7] Ibid., 56–57.
[8] Ibid., 60–62.
[9] Ibid., 68.
[10] Ibid.
[11] Ibid., 71–74.
[12] Ibid., 74.
[13] Christian Golder, "Mission and Aim of the Female Diaconate in the United States" in *Women and Religion in America,* 3 vols., ed. Rosemary R. Ruether and Rosemary S. Keller (San Francisco: Harper and Row, 1981), 1:270–71.
[14] Evangeline, *Daisy,* 77–78.
[15] Lois Neely, *Fire in His Bones* (Wheaton, Ill.: Tyndale House, 1982), 89.
[16] Evangeline, *Daisy,* 78–89.
[17] Oswald J. Smith, *The Story of My Life* (London: Marshall, Morgan and Scott, 1962), 47–48, 52, 61–62.
[18] Neely, *Fire in His Bones,* 93–94.
[19] Evangeline, *Daisy,* 91; Neely, *Fire in His Bones,* 96–98.
[20] Neely, *Fire in His Bones,* 100–102.
[21] Ibid., 107–8.
[22] Ibid., 121–23.

23 Neely, *Fire in His Bones*, 124–25; Smith, *The Story of My Life*, 76–80.
24 Smith, *The Story of My Life*, 82; Neely, *Fire in His Bones*, 134–35, 150.
25 Neely, *Fire in His Bones*, 140–41.
26 Evangeline, *Daisy*, 117.
27 Neely, *Fire in His Bones*, 141.
28 Evangeline, *Daisy*, 112–16.
29 Neely, *Fire in His Bones*, 151–55.
30 Oswald J. Smith, *The People's Church* (Toronto: Peoples Press, 1959), 86–87.
31 Neely, *Fire in His Bones*, 161, 167.
32 Ibid., 183, 201–6.
33 Ibid., 238–39.
34 Evangeline, *Daisy*, 218–19.
35 Neely, *Fire in His Bones*, 285–86.

Chapter 12. Catherine Marshall

1 Denise Turner, *Home Sweet Fishbowl: Confessions of a Minister's Wife* (Waco, Tex.: Word, 1982), 134.
2 Ibid., 57–58.
3 Frances Nordland, *The Unprivate Life of a Pastor's Wife* (Chicago: Moody Press, 1972), 106.
4 Catherine Marshall, *Beyond Our Selves* (New York: McGraw-Hill, 1961), 35–37, 39, 43.
5 Catherine Marshall, *A Man Called Peter* (New York: McGraw-Hill, 1951), 50–52; Paul W. Smart, "The Inner World of Catherine Marshall," *Christian Life* (February 1968): 41.
6 Marshall, *A Man Called Peter*, 53.
7 Catherine Marshall, *Meeting God at Every Turn* (Lincoln, Va.: Chosen Books, 1980), 75.
8 Marshall, *A Man Called Peter*, 45.
9 Ibid., 69, 73, 77, 97.
10 Ibid., 99–100.
11 Marshall, *Meeting God at Every Turn*, 83.
12 Marshall, *A Man Called Peter*, 101.
13 Ibid., 101–2.
14 Ibid., 115–16.
15 Catherine Marshall, *To Live Again* (New York: Avon, 1957), 101–3.
16 Marshall, *A Man Called Peter*, 117–18.
17 Ibid., 119.
18 Ibid., 136, 141.
19 Ibid., 214, 1–3.
20 Marshall, *To Live Again*, 11–12.
21 Ibid., 42–44.
22 Marshall, *Meeting God at Every Turn*, 113–14.
23 Marshall, *To Live Again*, 25.
24 Ibid., 47–48.
25 Ibid., 58, 94.
26 Marshall, *Beyond Our Selves*, xv.
27 Smart, "The Inner World of Catherine Marshall," 45.
28 Beth Spring, "Author Catherine Marshall Dies," *Christianity Today* 36 (22 April 1983): 38.

[29] Marshall, *To Live Again,* 169–71.

Chapter 13. Ruth Peale

[1] Ruth Senter, *So You're the Pastor's Wife* (Grand Rapids: Zondervan, 1979), 110–11.

[2] Frances Nordland, *The Unprivate Life of a Pastor's Wife* (Chicago: Moody Press, 1972), 119, 121.

[3] Betty J. Coble, *The Private Life of the Minister's Wife* (Nashville: Broadman, 1981), 106.

[4] Ruth Peale, *The Adventure of Being a Wife* (Englewood Cliffs: Prentice-Hall, 1971), 15.

[5] Ibid., 18.

[6] Arthur Gordon, *One Man's Way: The Story and Message of Norman Vincent Peale* (Englewood Cliffs: Prentice-Hall, 1972), 126–27.

[7] Norman Vincent Peale, *The True Joy of Positive Living* (New York: Ballantine, 1984), 105.

[8] Gordon, *One Man's Way,* 129.

[9] Norman Vincent Peale, *True Joy,* 105–6.

[10] Ruth Peale, *The Adventure of Being a Wife,* 24.

[11] Gordon, *One Man's Way,* 143, 166.

[12] Ruth Peale, *The Adventure of Being a Wife,* 29–30.

[13] Ibid., 63.

[14] Ibid., 63–65.

[15] Ibid., 30–31.

[16] Ibid., 55.

[17] Ibid.

[18] Ibid., 29.

[19] Ibid., 34–35.

[20] Norman Vincent Peale, *True Joy,* 163, 177, 185, 187.

[21] Ibid., 123, 130.

[22] Gordon, *One Man's Way,* 155.

[23] Norman Vincent Peale, *True Joy,* 130–31.

[24] Ibid., 132.

[25] Ruth Peale, *The Adventure of Being a Wife,* 147–48; Norman Vincent Peale, *True Joy,* 150.

[26] Ruth Peale, *The Adventure of Being a Wife,* 149–50.

[27] Ibid., 155.

[28] Ibid., 157.

[29] Ibid., 236, 238.

[30] Gordon, *One Man's Way,* 237.

Chapter 14. Jill Briscoe

[1] Alice Taylor, *How to Be a Minister's Wife and Love It* (Grand Rapids: Zondervan, 1968), 20–21.

[2] Clayton Bell, "A Look at Grief," *Leadership* 1 (Fall 1980): 42, 51.

[3] Jill Briscoe, *Queen of Hearts: The Role of Today's Woman* (Old Tappan, N.J.: Fleming H. Revell, 1984), 132–33.

[4] Jill Briscoe, *Thank You for Being a Friend* (Garden City, N.Y.: Doubleday, 1980), 109.

[5] Ibid., 112.

[6] Ibid., 115.

[7] Jill Briscoe, *There's a Snake in My Garden* (Grand Rapids: Zondervan, 1975), 38–40.

[8] Ibid., 46–48.

[9] Ibid., 52–59.

[10] Ibid., 61–64.

[11] Briscoe, *Thank You,* 177.

[12] Stuart Briscoe, "The Biblical Woman: We've Buried a Treasure," *Moody Monthly* (February 1983): 6.

[13] Briscoe, *There's a Snake,* 89.

[14] Ibid., 91.

[15] Ibid., 92.

[16] Ibid., 93.

[17] Briscoe, *Thank You,* 179.

[18] Briscoe, *There's a Snake,* 100–101.

[19] Ibid., 106–8.

[20] Ibid., 109.

[21] Ibid., 112.

[22] Ibid., 113.

[23] Ibid., 113–14.

[24] Ibid., 115.

[25] Ibid., 121–22.

[26] Ibid., 122–23.

Conclusion

[1] Flo Whyard, ed., *Five Pioneer Women of the Anglican Church in the Yukon* (Whitehorse, Yukon: Willow Printers, 1983), 8, 17, 20.

[2] "In Memoriam: Jessie Bartlett Hess, 1881–1969," unpublished paper.

• Bibliography •

Bainton, Roland H. *Here I Stand: A Life of Martin Luther*. New York: Mentor Books, 1950.

————. *Women of the Reformation in Germany and Italy*. Minneapolis: Augsburg, 1971.

Beecher, Eunice. "Mr. and Mrs. Beecher's Plans." *Ladies' Home Journal* 9 (February 1892).

Beecher, William C., and Rev. Samuel Scoville, assisted by Mrs. Henry Ward Beecher. *A Biography of Henry Ward Beecher*. New York: Charles L. Webster, 1888.

Bell, Clayton. "A Look at Grief." *Leadership* 1 (Fall 1980).

Benson, Joseph. *The Life of the Rev. John W. de la Fléchère*. New York: Carlton and Phillips, 1853.

Briscoe, Jill. *Queen of Hearts: The Role of Today's Woman*. Old Tappan, N.J.: Fleming H. Revell, 1984.

————. *Thank You for Being a Friend*. Garden City, N.Y.: Doubleday, 1980.

————. *There's a Snake in My Garden*. Grand Rapids: Zondervan, 1975.

Briscoe, Stuart. "The Biblical Woman: We've Buried a Treasure." *Moody Monthly* (February 1983): 5–6.

Brown, Earl Kent. *Women of Mr. Wesley's Methodism*. New York: Edwin Mellen, 1983.

Burns, Jabez. *Life of Mrs. Fletcher*. London: Joseph Smith, 1853.

Chapman, J. Wilbur. *The Life and Work of Dwight L. Moody*. New York: Noble, 1900.

Chrisman, Mariam V. "Women of the Reformation in Strasbourg, 1490–1530." *Archive for Reformation History* 63 (1972).

Clark, Clifford E. Jr. *Henry Ward Beecher: Spokesman for Middle-Class America*. Urbana: University of Illinois, 1978.

Coble, Betty J. *The Private Life of a Minister's Wife*. Nashville: Broadman, 1981.

Conwell, Russell H. *Life of Charles Haddon Spurgeon*. N.p.: Edgewood, 1892.

Curtis, Richard K. *They Called Him Mister Moody*. Grand Rapids: Wm. B. Eerdmans, 1962.

Dallimore, Arnold. *Spurgeon*. Chicago: Moody Press, 1984.

Daniels, W. H. *Moody: His Words, Works, and Workers*. New York: Nelson and Phillips, 1977.

Day, Richard Ellsworth. *The Shadow of the Broad Brim: The Life Story of Charles Haddon Spurgeon, Heir of the Puritans*. Valley Forge, Pa.: Judson Press, 1934.

Deen, Edith. *Great Women of the Christian Faith*. New York: Harper and Row, 1959.

Dodds, Elizabeth D. *Marriage to a Difficult Man: The "Uncommon Union" of Jonathan and Sarah Edwards*. Philadelphia: Westminster, 1971.

Dwight, S. E. *The Life of President Edwards*. New York: G. and C. and H. Carvill, 1830.

Edwards, Jonathan. "Sarah Pierrpont." *Jonathan Edwards, Representative Selections*. Rev. ed., edited by Clarence H. Faust and Thomas H. Johnson. New York: Hill and Wang, 1962.

Evangeline, Hope. *Daisy*. Grand Rapids: Baker, 1978.

Findlay, James F., Jr. *Dwight L. Moody: American Evangelist, 1837–1899*. Chicago: University of Chicago Press, 1969.

Fowler, C. H. *D. L. Moody and His Work*. N.p.: n.p., 1875.

Friedenthal, Richard. *Luther: His Life and Times*. Translated by John Nowell. New York: Harcourt Brace, 1970.

Fulton, J. D. *Spurgeon, Our Ally*. Chicago: H. J. Smith, 1892.

Golder, Christian. "Mission and Aim of the Female Diaconate in the United States." In *Women and Religion in America*. Vol. 1, *The Nineteenth Century*, edited by Rosemary R. Ruether and Rosemary S. Keller. San Francisco: Harper and Row, 1981.

Gordon, Arthur. *One Man's Way: The Story and Message of Norman Vincent Peale*. Englewood Cliffs, N.J.: Prentice-Hall, 1972.

Harkness, Georgia. *John Calvin: The Man and His Ethics*. Nashville: Abingdon, 1958.

Harmon, Rebecca L. *Susanna: Mother of the Wesleys*. Nashville: Abingdon, 1968.

Hassey, Janette. *No Time for Silence: Evangelical Women in Public Ministry Around the Turn of the Century.* Grand Rapids: Zondervan, 1986.

Hibben, Paxton. *Henry Ward Beecher: An American Portrait.* New York: George H. Doran, 1927.

Hyma, Albert. *Life of John Calvin.* Grand Rapids: Wm. B. Eerdmans, 1943.

"In Memoriam: Jessie Bartlett Hess, 1881–1969," unpublished paper, n.d.

Kleinhans, Theodore J. *Martin Luther: Saint and Sinner.* London: Marshall, Morgan and Scott, 1959.

Kruppa, Patricia S. *Charles Haddon Spurgeon: A Preacher's Progress.* New York: Garland, 1982.

Mace, David, and Vera Mace. *What's Happening to Clergy Marriages?* Nashville: Abingdon, 1980.

Mains, Karen Burton. *Open Heart, Open Home.* Elgin, Ill.: David C. Cook, 1976.

Marshall, Catherine. *Beyond Our Selves.* New York: McGraw-Hill, 1961.

————. *A Man Called Peter.* New York: McGraw-Hill, 1951.

————. *Meeting God at Every Turn.* Lincoln, Va.: Chosen Books, 1980.

————. *To Live Again.* New York: Avon Books, 1957.

MacDonald, Gail. *High Call, High Privilege.* Wheaton, Ill.: Tyndale House, 1981.

McGraw, Gerald E. *The Doctrine of Sanctification in the Published Writings of Albert Benjamin Simpson.* Ph.D. diss., New York University, 1986.

McKim, Donald K. "Disturber of the Peace: A Profile of Katherine Zell, Unknown Reformer." *Eternity* (June 1984).

Moore, Henry. *The Life of Mrs. Mary Fletcher.* New York: Hunt and Eaton, 1817.

Murray, Iain, ed. *The Early Years.* London: Banner of Truth Trust, 1962.

Needham, George C. *The Life and Labors of Charles H. Spurgeon.* Boston: D. L. Guernsey, 1884.

Neely, Lois. *Fire in His Bones.* Wheaton, Ill.: Tyndale House, 1982.

Niklaus, Robert L.; John S. Sawin; and Samuel J. Stoesz. *All for Jesus: God at Work in the Christian and Missionary Alliance Over One Hundred Years.* Camp Hill, Pa.: Christian Publications, 1986.

Nordland, Frances. *The Unprivate Life of a Pastor's Wife.* Chicago: Moody Press, 1972.

Oden, Marilyn Brown. *The Minister's Wife: Person or Position?* Nashville: Abingdon, 1966.

O'Faolain. Julia, and Lauro Martines, eds. *Not in God's Image.* New York: Harper and Row, 1973.

Olson, Bessie. *John Fletcher, the Great Saint.* Des Moines: Boone Publishing, 1944.

Parker, T. H. L. *John Calvin: A Biography.* Philadelphia: Westminster, 1975.

Parrott, Lora Lee. *How To Be a Preacher's Wife and Like It.* Grand Rapids: Zondervan, 1956.

Peale, Norman Vincent. *The True Joy of Positive Living.* New York: Ballantine Books, 1984.

Peale, Ruth. *The Adventure of Being a Wife.* Englewood Cliffs, N.J.: Prentice-Hall, 1971.

Peck, M. Scott. *The Road Less Traveled: A New Psychology of Love, Traditional Values and Spiritual Growth.* New York: Simon and Schuster, 1978.

Pentecost, Dorothy Harrison. *The Pastor's Wife and the Church.* Chicago: Moody Press, 1964.

Peterson, William J. "Idelette: John Calvin's Search for the Right Wife." *Christian History* 5, no. 4 (1986): 12–15.

Pollock, J. C. *Moody: A Biographical Portrait of the Pacesetter in Modern Mass Evangelism.* New York: Macmillan, 1963.

Porterfield, Amanda. *Feminine Spirituality in America: From Sarah Edwards to Martha Graham.* Philadelphia: Temple University Press, 1980.

Powell, Emma Moody. *Heavenly Destiny: The Life Story of Mrs. D. L. Moody.* Chicago: Moody Press, 1943.

Ross, Charlotte. *Who Is the Minister's Wife?: A Search for Personal Fulfillment.* Philadelphia: Westminster, 1980.

Schaff, Philip. *History of the Christian Church.* Vol. 8. Grand Rapids: Wm. B. Eerdmans, 1979.

Schwiebert, E. G. *Luther and His Times.* St. Louis: Concordia, 1950.

Senter, Ruth. *So You're the Pastor's Wife.* Grand Rapids: Zondervan, 1979.

Sinclair, Donna. *The Pastor's Wife Today.* Nashville: Abingdon, 1981.

Smart, Paul W. "The Inner World of Catherine Marshall." *Christian Life* (February 1968): 22–25, 40–45.

Smith, Oswald J. *The People's Church.* Toronto: The Peoples Press, 1959.

————. *The Story of My Life.* London: Marshall, Morgan and Scott, 1962.

Spring, Beth. "Author Catherine Marshall Dies." *Christianity Today* 36 (22 April 1983): 36–38.

Spurgeon, C. H. *Autobiography.* Vol. 1, *The Early Years, 1834–1859.* London: Banner of Truth Trust, 1962.

Spurgeon, Susannah, and J. W. Harrald, comp. *C. H. Spurgeon's Autobiography.* 4 vols. London: Passmore and Alabaster, 1897.

Sweet, Leonard I. *The Minister's Wife: Her Role in Nineteenth-Century American Evangelicalism.* Philadelphia: Temple University Press, 1983.

Taft, Zachariah. *Biographical Sketches of the Lives and Public Ministry of Various Holy Women.* 2 vols. London: Dershaw, 1825; Leeds: Cullingworth, 1828.

Taylor, Alice. *How to Be a Minister's Wife and Love It.* Grand Rapids: Zondervan, 1968.

Thompson, A. E. *The Life of A. B. Simpson.* New York: Christian Alliance Publishing Co., 1920.

Tozer, A. W. *Wingspread: A. B. Simpson, A Study in Spiritual Altitude.* Harrisburg: Christian Publications, 1943.

Turner, Denise. *Home Sweet Fishbowl: Confessions of a Minister's Wife.* Waco, Tex.: Word, 1982.

Tuttle, Robert G., Jr. *John Wesley: His Life and Theology.* Grand Rapids: Zondervan, 1978.

Van Halsema, Thea B. *This Was John Calvin.* Grand Rapids: Baker, 1981.

Walker, Williston. *John Calvin: The Organizer of Reformed Protestantism, 1509–1564.* New York: Schocken, 1969.

Wallace, Charles, Jr. "Susanna Wesley's Spirituality: The Freedom of a Christian Woman." *Methodist History* 22 (April 1984): 158–73.

Waller, Altina L. *Reverend Beecher and Mrs. Tilton: Sex and Class in Victorian America.* Amherst: University of Massachusetts Press, 1982.

Wesley, John. *The Works of John Wesley.* 13 vols. Grand Rapids: Zondervan, 1958–59.

Whyard, Flo, ed. *Five Pioneer Women of the Anglican Church in the Yukon.* Whitehorse, Yukon: Willow Printers, 1983.

Winslow, Ola Elizabeth. *Jonathan Edwards, 1703–1758: A Biography.* New York: Macmillan, 1940.

Wright, Naomi Taylor, with Dick Bohrer. "Let's Let Women Counsel Women." *Moody Monthly* (November 1980): 41–42.

• Index •